IMMIGRATION IN THE 21ST CENTURY:
POLITICAL, SOCIAL AND ECONOMIC ISSUES

UNACCOMPANIED ALIEN CHILDREN IN THE UNITED STATES

ISSUES AND TRENDS

IMMIGRATION IN THE 21ST CENTURY: POLITICAL, SOCIAL AND ECONOMIC ISSUES

Additional books in this series can be found on Nova's website under the Series tab.

Additional e-books in this series can be found on Nova's website under the e-book tab.

IMMIGRATION IN THE 21ST CENTURY: POLITICAL, SOCIAL AND ECONOMIC ISSUES

UNACCOMPANIED ALIEN CHILDREN IN THE UNITED STATES

ISSUES AND TRENDS

PAUL SNIDER
EDITOR

nova publishers
New York

For permission to use material from this book please contact us:
Telephone 631-231-7269; Fax 631-231-8175
Web Site: http://www.novapublishers.com

Library of Congress Cataloging-in-Publication Data

ISBN: 978-1-63321-832-1

Published by Nova Science Publishers, Inc. † New York

CONTENTS

PREFACE

The book opens with an analysis of the data of the recent surge in UAC crossing the border. It then discusses current policy on the treatment, care, and custody of the population. The processing and treatment of UAC is detailed, with a discussion of each agency that is involved with the population. The book then discusses both Administrative and Congressional action to deal with the current crisis. As this issue is still emerging, the book concludes with a series of questions related to UAC that remain unanswered.

Chapter 1 – The number of unaccompanied alien children (UAC) arriving in the United States has reached alarming numbers that has strained the system put in place over the past decade to handle such cases. UAC are defined in statute as children who lack lawful immigration status in the United States, who are under the age of 18, and who are without a parent or legal guardian in the United States or no parent or legal guardian in the United States is available to provide care and physical custody. Two statutes and a legal settlement most directly affect U.S. policy for the treatment and administrative processing of UAC: the *Flores Settlement Agreement* of 1997; the Homeland Security Act of 2002; and the Trafficking Victims Protection Reauthorization Act of 2008.

Several agencies in the Department of Homeland Security (DHS) and the Department of Health and Human Services' (HHS) Office of Refugee Resettlement (ORR) share responsibilities for the processing, treatment, and placement of UAC. DHS Customs and Border Protection apprehends and detains UAC arrested at the border while Immigration and Customs Enforcement (ICE) handles the transfer and repatriation responsibilities. ICE also apprehends UAC in the interior of the country and is responsible for representing the government in removal proceedings. HHS is responsible for coordinating and implementing the care and placement of UAC in appropriate custody.

Four countries account for almost all of the UAC cases (El Salvador, Guatemala, Honduras, and Mexico) and much of the recent increase has come from El Salvador, Guatemala, and Honduras. In FY2009, Mexican UAC accounted for 82% of 19,668 UAC apprehensions, while the other three Central American countries accounted for 17%. By the first eight months of FY2014, the proportions had almost reversed, with Mexican UAC comprising only 25% of the 47,017 UAC apprehensions, and UAC from the three Central American countries comprising 73%.

Both the Administration and Congress have begun to take action to respond to the surge in UAC coming across the border. The Administration has developed a working group to coordinate the efforts of the various agencies involved in responding to the issue. It also has opened additional shelters and holding facilities to accommodate the large number of UAC apprehended at the border. The Administration has also announced plans to provide funding to the affected Central American countries for a variety of programs and security-related initiatives. Relatedly, Congress is considering funding increases for HHS and DHS.

Chapter 2 – Since FY2008, the growth in the number of unaccompanied alien children (UAC) from Mexico, El Salvador, Guatemala, and Honduras seeking to enter the United States has increased substantially. Total unaccompanied child apprehensions increased from about 8,000 in FY2008 to 52,000 in the first 8 1/2 months of FY2014. Since 2012, children from El Salvador, Guatemala, and Honduras (Central America's "northern triangle") account for almost all of this increase. Apprehension trends for these three countries are similar and diverge sharply from those for Mexican children. Unaccompanied child migrants' motives for migrating to the United States are often multifaceted and difficult to measure analytically.

Four recent out-migration-related factors distinguishing northern triangle Central American countries are high violent crime rates, poor economic conditions fueled by relatively low economic growth rates, high rates of poverty, and the presence of transnational gangs. In 2012, the homicide rate per 100,000 inhabitants stood at 90.4 in Honduras (the highest in the world), 41.2 in El Salvador, and 39.9 in Guatemala. International Monetary Fund reports show economic growth rates in the northern triangle countries in 2013 ranging from 1.6% to 3.5%, relatively low compared with other Central American countries. About 45% of Salvadorans, 55% of Guatemalans, and 67% of Hondurans live in poverty. Surveys in 2013 indicate that almost half of all unaccompanied children experienced serious harm or threats by organized criminal groups or state actors, and one-fifth experienced domestic abuse.

In 2011, Mexico passed legislation to improve migration management and ensure the rights of migrants transiting the country. According to many migration experts, implementation of the laws has been uneven. Some have questioned whether passage of such legislation has affected in some way the recent flows of unaccompanied children. However, the impact of such laws remains unclear.

Although economic opportunity may motivate some unaccompanied children to migrate to the United States, labor market conditions for low-skilled minority youth have worsened in recent years, even as industrial sectors employing low-skilled workers enjoy improved economic prospects. Educational opportunities may also provide a motivating factor to migration as perceptions of free and safe education may be widespread among the young. Family reunification is reported to be one of the key motives of unaccompanied children. Many have family members among the sizable Salvadoran, Guatemalan, and Honduran foreign-born populations residing in the United States.

While the impacts of actual and perceived U.S. immigration policies have been widely debated, it remains unclear if, and how, specific immigration policies have motivated children to migrate to the United States. Misperceptions about U.S. policies may be a contributing factor. The existence of long-standing humanitarian relief policies confounds causal links between them and the recent surge in unaccompanied children. A notable and recent exception is revised humanitarian relief provisions for unaccompanied children included in the Trafficking Victims Protection Reauthorization Act (TVPRA) of 2008, which affects asylum claims, trafficking victim protections, and eligibility for Special Immigrant Juvenile Status. Some argue that unaccompanied children and their families falsely believe they would be covered under the Deferred Action for Childhood Arrivals (DACA) initiative and legalization provisions in proposed comprehensive immigration reform (CIR) legislation.

Chapter 3 – Recent reports about the increasing number of alien minors apprehended at the U.S. border without a parent or legal guardian have prompted numerous questions about so-called unaccompanied alien children (UACs). Some of these questions pertain to the numbers of children involved, their reasons for coming to the United States, and current and potential responses of the federal government and other entities to their arrival. Other questions concern the interpretation and interplay of various federal statutes and regulations, administrative and judicial decisions, and settlement agreements pertaining to alien minors. This report addresses the latter questions, providing general and relatively brief answers to 14 frequently asked questions regarding UACs.

Some of the questions and answers in the report provide basic definitions and background information relevant to discussions of UACs, such as the legal definition of *unaccompanied alien child*; the difference between being a UAC and having Special Immigrant Juvenile (SIJ) status; the terms and enforcement of the *Flores* settlement agreement; and why UACs encountered at a port of entry—as some recent arrivals have been—are not turned away on the grounds that they are inadmissible. Other questions and answers explore which federal agencies have primary responsibility for maintaining custody of alien children without immigration status; removal proceedings against such children; the release of alien minors from federal custody; the "best interest of the child" standard; and whether UACs could obtain asylum due to gang violence in their home countries. Yet other questions and answers address whether UACs have a right to counsel at the government's expense; their ability under the Vienna Convention on Consular Relations to have consular officials of their home country notified of their detention; and whether UACs are eligible for inclusion in the Obama Administration's Deferred Action for Childhood Arrivals (DACA) initiative.

Chapter 4 – Immigration reform has been hotly debated in recent years. Broadly construed, it encompasses a range of issues, including the highly controversial question of legalizing large numbers of unauthorized immigrants in the United States. A historically less controversial, more targeted legalization proposal has been included in the "DREAM Act," legislation that seeks to enable certain unauthorized aliens who entered the United States as children to obtain legal immigration status. The name DREAM Act derives from the bill title, Development, Relief, and Education for Alien Minors Act, but it refers more broadly to measures to provide immigration relief to unauthorized students, whether or not particular bills carry that name.

Unauthorized aliens in the United States are able to receive free public education through high school. They may experience difficulty obtaining higher education, however, for several reasons. Among these reasons is a provision enacted in 1996 that prohibits states from granting unauthorized aliens certain postsecondary educational benefits on the basis of state residence, unless equal benefits are made available to all U.S. citizens. This prohibition is commonly understood to apply to the granting of "in-state" residency status for tuition purposes. Unauthorized alien students also are not eligible for federal student financial aid. More broadly, as unauthorized aliens, they typically are not legally allowed to work and are subject to being removed from the country.

Multiple DREAM Act bills have been introduced in recent Congresses to address the unauthorized student population. Most have proposed a two-prong approach of repealing the 1996 provision and enabling some unauthorized alien students to become U.S. legal permanent residents (LPRs) through an immigration procedure known as cancellation of removal. While there are other options for dealing with this population, this report deals exclusively with the DREAM Act approach in light of the considerable congressional interest in it.

In the 111th Congress, the House approved DREAM Act language as part of an unrelated bill, the Removal Clarification Act of 2010 (H.R. 5281). The Senate, however, failed to invoke cloture on a motion to agree to the House-passed DREAM Act amendment, and the bill died at the end of the Congress. The House-approved language differed in key respects from earlier versions of the DREAM Act. Bills to legalize the status of unauthorized alien students were again introduced in the 112th Congress.

In 2012, in the absence of congressional action on DREAM Act legislation, the Obama Administration announced that certain individuals who entered the United States as children and meet other criteria would be considered for relief from removal. Under a Department of Homeland Security (DHS) memorandum, these individuals can apply for consideration of deferred action for childhood arrivals (or DACA, as the program is known). Successful applicants are granted deferred action for two years, subject to renewal, and can apply for employment authorization.

DREAM Act legislation has been considered in the 113th Congress as part of comprehensive immigration reform bills. The Senate-passed Border Security, Economic Opportunity, and Immigration Modernization Act (S. 744) includes DREAM Act provisions. The same DREAM Act language is included in a related bill with the same name introduced in the House (H.R. 15). The DREAM Act provisions are integrated with the broader legalization provisions in these bills. As of this writing, no stand-alone DREAM Act bills have been introduced in the 113th Congress.

Chapter 5 – For several years, some Members of Congress have favored "comprehensive immigration reform" (CIR), a label that commonly refers to omnibus legislation that includes increased border security and immigration enforcement, expanded employment eligibility verification, revision of nonimmigrant visas and legal permanent immigration, and legalization for some unauthorized aliens residing in the country. The omnibus legislative approach contrasts with incremental revisions of the Immigration and Nationality Act (INA) and other immigration laws that would address some but not all of these elements, and with sequential reforms that would tackle border security and interior enforcement provisions prior to revising legal immigration or enacting legalization pathways.

Leaders in both chambers have identified immigration as a legislative priority in the 113th Congress. While the House Committee on the Judiciary has ordered reported several distinct pieces of legislation that aim to reform immigration law thus far in the 113th Congress, the debate in the Senate has focused on a single CIR bill: the Border Security, Economic Opportunity, and Immigration Modernization Act (S. 744). This report briefly summarizes major provisions of S. 744, which the Senate amended and passed by a yea-nay vote of 68-32 on June 27, 2013.

CRS's analysis focuses on eight major policy areas that encompass the U.S. immigration debate: comprehensive reform "triggers" and funding; border security; interior enforcement; employment eligibility verification and worksite enforcement; legalization of unauthorized aliens; immigrant visas; nonimmigrant visas; and humanitarian provisions.

This report provides a concise summary of S. 744 related to each of these issues.

In: Unaccompanied Alien Children in the U.S. ISBN: 978-1-63321-832-1
Editor: Paul Snider

Chapter 1

UNACCOMPANIED ALIEN CHILDREN: AN OVERVIEW*

Lisa Seghetti, Alison Siskin and Ruth Ellen Wasem

SUMMARY

The number of unaccompanied alien children (UAC) arriving in the United States has reached alarming numbers that has strained the system put in place over the past decade to handle such cases. UAC are defined in statute as children who lack lawful immigration status in the United States, who are under the age of 18, and who are without a parent or legal guardian in the United States or no parent or legal guardian in the United States is available to provide care and physical custody. Two statutes and a legal settlement most directly affect U.S. policy for the treatment and administrative processing of UAC: the *Flores Settlement Agreement* of 1997; the Homeland Security Act of 2002; and the Trafficking Victims Protection Reauthorization Act of 2008.

Several agencies in the Department of Homeland Security (DHS) and the Department of Health and Human Services' (HHS) Office of Refugee Resettlement (ORR) share responsibilities for the processing, treatment, and placement of UAC. DHS Customs and Border Protection apprehends and detains UAC arrested at the border while Immigration and Customs Enforcement (ICE) handles the transfer and repatriation responsibilities.

---

* This is an edited, reformatted and augmented version of a Congressional Research Service publication R43599, prepared for Members and Committees of Congress, dated June 23, 2014.

ICE also apprehends UAC in the interior of the country and is responsible for representing the government in removal proceedings. HHS is responsible for coordinating and implementing the care and placement of UAC in appropriate custody.

Four countries account for almost all of the UAC cases (El Salvador, Guatemala, Honduras, and Mexico) and much of the recent increase has come from El Salvador, Guatemala, and Honduras. In FY2009, Mexican UAC accounted for 82% of 19,668 UAC apprehensions, while the other three Central American countries accounted for 17%. By the first eight months of FY2014, the proportions had almost reversed, with Mexican UAC comprising only 25% of the 47,017 UAC apprehensions, and UAC from the three Central American countries comprising 73%.

Both the Administration and Congress have begun to take action to respond to the surge in UAC coming across the border. The Administration has developed a working group to coordinate the efforts of the various agencies involved in responding to the issue. It also has opened additional shelters and holding facilities to accommodate the large number of UAC apprehended at the border. The Administration has also announced plans to provide funding to the affected Central American countries for a variety of programs and security-related initiatives. Relatedly, Congress is considering funding increases for HHS and DHS.

BACKGROUND

There has been a large increase in the number of unaccompanied alien children (UAC) apprehended along the Southwest boarder, which has placed a strain on several agencies and their resources. During a recent hearing on the topic, Congressional members, like the Administration, characterized the issue as a humanitarian crisis.[1] Overwhelmingly the children are coming from three Central American countries,[2] and Mexico. They are reportedly coming for economic opportunities, escaping violence in their home countries, and to be reunited with parents or other family members who are living in the United States.[3] Critics of the Obama Administration, however, assert that the recent surge in UAC fleeing their home countries is due to a perception of relaxed U.S. immigration policy towards children.[4]

Unaccompanied alien[5] children (UAC) are defined in statute as children who lack lawful immigration status in the United States,[6] are under the age of 18, are without a parent or legal guardian in the United States, or no parent or legal guardian in the United States is available to provide care and physical custody.[7] They most often arrive at United States ports of entry or are apprehended along the southwestern border with Mexico. Less frequently they are apprehended in the interior and determined to be a juvenile[8] and unaccompanied.[9] Although most of these children are aged 14 or older, recently there has been an increase in the apprehension of UAC under the age of 13.[10]

The report opens with an analysis of the data of the recent surge in UAC crossing the border. It then discusses current policy on the treatment, care, and custody of the population. The processing and treatment of UAC is detailed, with a discussion of each agency that is involved with the population. The report then discusses both Administrative and Congressional action to deal with the current crisis. As this issue is still emerging, the report concludes with a series of questions related to UAC that remain unanswered.

SCOPE OF THE PROBLEM

Overall, the number of UAC apprehended by the Border Patrol has increased significantly over the past five years, and most of the increase comes from three countries: El Salvador, Guatemala, and Honduras.[11] As of the end of May, the Border Patrol apprehended more UAC than in any of the previous five years, and had apprehended almost twice as many UAC as in FY2012.

According to the Administration, in FY2014 there has been an increase in the number of UAC who are girls and the number of UAC who are under the age of 13. Because CRS was unable to get data to illustrate this change, it is unclear whether the increase in girls and in children under 13 in the UAC population is simply because the number of all UAC has increased, or if the number of girls and children under 13 has increased as a proportion of all UAC.

Nationals of Guatemala, Honduras, El Salvador, and Mexico account for almost all unaccompanied alien children apprehended at the Mexico-U.S. border, as *Figure 1* shows. Flows of UAC from Mexico rose substantially in FY2009 and have remained rather steady. UAC from Guatemala, Honduras, and El Salvador account for the surge beginning in FY2012. In FY2009, Mexican UAC accounted for 82% of 19,668 UAC apprehensions, while the other three Central American countries accounted for 17%. By the first eight months of FY2014, the proportions had almost reversed, with Mexican UAC comprising only 25% of the 47,017 UAC apprehensions, and UAC from the three Central American countries comprising 73%.

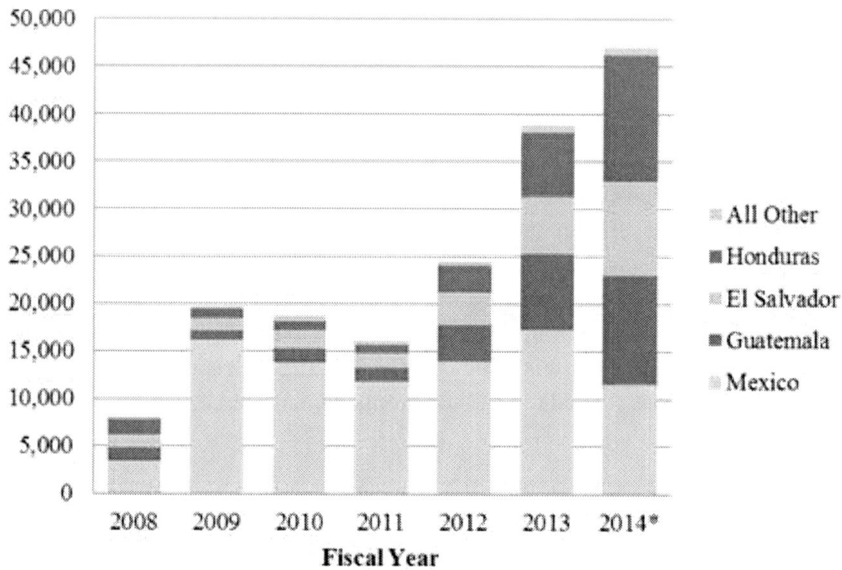

Source: For FY2008-FY2013: U.S. Department of Homeland Security, United States Border Patrol, Juvenile and Adult Apprehensions—Fiscal Year 2013. For FY2014, unpublished data provided by Customs and Border Protection to CRS.

Notes: FY2014 figures are October 1, 2013 to May 31, 2014, representing 2/3 of a fiscal year.

Figure 1. UAC Apprehensions by Country of Origin, FY2008-FY2014.

CURRENT POLICY[12]

Two laws and a settlement discussed below most directly affect U.S. policy for the treatment and administrative processing of UAC: the Flores Settlement Agreement of 1997; the Homeland Security Act of 2002; and the Trafficking Victims Protection Reauthorization Act of 2008.

During the 1980s, allegations of UAC mistreatment by the former Immigration and Naturalization Service (INS)[13] caused a series of lawsuits against the government that eventually resulted in the *Flores Settlement Agreement* (*Flores Agreement*) in 1997.[14] The *Flores Agreement* established a nationwide policy for the detention, treatment, and release of UAC and recognized the particular vulnerability of UAC while detained without a parent or legal guardian present.[15] It required that immigration officials detaining minors provide (1) food and drinking water; (2) medical assistance in emergencies; (3) toilets and sinks; (4) adequate temperature control and ventilation; (5) adequate supervision to protect minors from others; and (6) separation from unrelated adults whenever possible. For several years following the *Flores Agreement*, criticism continued over whether the INS had fully implemented the regulations that had been drafted.[16]

Five years later, the Homeland Security Act of 2002 (HSA; P.L. 107-296) divided responsibilities for the processing and treatment of UAC between the newly created Department of Homeland Security (DHS) and the Department of Health and Human Services' (HHS) Office of Refugee Resettlement (ORR). The HSA assigned apprehension, transfer, and repatriation responsibilities to DHS. To HHS, the law assigned responsibility for coordinating and implementing the care and placement of UAC in appropriate custody; reunifying UAC with their parents abroad if appropriate; maintaining and publishing a list of legal services available to UAC; and collecting statistical information on UAC, among other things.[17] The HSA also established a statutory definition of UAC as unauthorized minors without the accompaniment of a parent or legal guardian. Despite these developments, criticism that the *Flores Agreement* had not been fully implemented continued.

In response to ongoing concerns that UAC who were apprehended by the Border Patrol were not being adequately screened to see if there were a reason that they should not be returned to their home country, Congress passed the William Wilberforce Trafficking Victims Protection Reauthorization Act of 2008 (TVPRA, P.L. 110-457). The TVPRA directed the Secretary of DHS, in conjunction with other federal agencies, to develop policies and procedures to ensure that UAC in the United States are safely repatriated to their country of nationality or of last habitual residence. The section set forth special rules for UAC from contiguous countries (i.e., Mexico and Canada), allowing such children, under certain circumstances, to return to Mexico or Canada without additional penalties, and directing the Secretary of State to negotiate agreements with Mexico and Canada to manage the repatriation process. Unaccompanied alien children from countries other than Mexico or Canada—along with UAC from those countries who are apprehended away from the border—are to be transferred to the care and custody of the Department of Health and Human Services (HHS) and placed in formal removal proceedings. The TVPRA requires that children from contiguous countries be screened within 48 hours of being apprehended to determine whether they should be returned to their country or transferred to HHS and placed in removal proceedings.

PROCESSING AND TREATMENT OF UAC APPREHENDED

Several DHS agencies are involved in apprehending, processing, and repatriating UAC, while the Department of Health and Human Services (HHS) is responsible for the care and custody of UAC. The Executive Office of Immigration Review (EOIR) in the U.S. Department of Justice conducts the immigration removal proceedings.

Customs and Border Protection (CBP) apprehends, processes, and detains the majority of UAC arrested along U.S. borders. Immigration and Customs Enforcement (ICE) physically transports UAC from CBP to HHS Office of Refugee Resettlement (HHS-ORR) custody. HHS-ORR is responsible for detaining and sheltering UAC who are from non-contiguous countries and those from contiguous countries (i.e., Canada and Mexico) for whom there is a concern that they may be victims of trafficking or have an asylum claim, while they await an immigration hearing. U.S. Citizenship and Immigration Services is responsible for the initial adjudication of asylum applications filed by UAC. The Executive Office of Immigration Review (EOIR) in the U.S. Department of Justice conducts the immigration proceedings that determine whether the UAC is allowed to remain in the United States or is deported to his or her home country. If a UAC is ordered removed from the United States, ICE is responsible for returning the alien to his/her home country. The following sections discuss the role of these federal agencies in apprehending, processing, detaining, and repatriating UAC.

Customs and Border Protection

The Office of Border Patrol (OBP)[18] and the Office of Field Operations (OFO)[19] are responsible for apprehending and processing UAC that come through a port of entry (POE) or are found at or near the border.[20] UAC that are apprehended between POEs are transported to Border Patrol stations, and if they are apprehended at POEs, they are escorted to CBP secondary screening areas. In both cases, when CBP confirms that juveniles have entered the country illegally and unaccompanied, they are considered UAC and processed for immigration violations, and the appropriate consulate is notified that the juvenile is being detained by DHS.

The Border Patrol apprehends the majority of UAC at or near the border. They also process UAC.[21] With the exception of Mexican and Canadian UAC who meet a set of criteria discussed below, the Border Patrol has to turn UAC over to ICE for transport to HHS-ORR within 72 hours.[22] Up until 2008, the Border Patrol, as a matter of policy and practice, returned Mexican UAC to Mexico under *voluntary departure*.[23] Under this practice, Mexican UAC were removed through the nearest POE and turned over to a Mexican official within twenty-four hours and during daylight.

As mentioned, the TVPRA required the Secretary of Homeland Security, in conjunction with the Secretary of State, the Attorney General, and the Secretary of HHS, to develop policies and procedures to ensure that UAC are safely repatriated to their country of nationality or last habitual residence. Of particular significance, the TVPRA required CBP to follow certain criteria for UAC that are nationals or habitual residents from a contiguous country (i.e., Canada and Mexico). In these cases, within 48 hours CBP personnel must screen the UAC to determine the following:

- that the UAC has not been a victim of a severe form of trafficking in persons and that there is no credible evidence that the minor is at risk should the minor be returned to his country of nationality or of last habitual residence;
- that the UAC does not have a possible claim to asylum; and
- that the UAC is able to make an independent decision to voluntarily return to his country of nationality or of last habitual residence.[24]

If, after assessing the UAC, CBP personnel determine the minor to be inadmissible under the Immigration and Nationality Act,[25] they can permit the minor to withdraw his application for admission[26] through *voluntary departure* and return the minor to his country of nationality or of last habitual residence.

The TVPRA contains a number of specific safeguards for the treatment of UAC while in the care and custody of CBP and it also provides guidance for CBP personnel on returning a minor to his country of nationality or of last habitual residence. It also requires the Secretary of State to negotiate agreements with the contiguous countries with respect to the repatriation of their UAC. The agreements would serve as a protection from trafficking and, at minimum, are required to include provisions pertaining to (1) the hand-off of the minor children to an appropriate government official; (2) a prohibition against returning UAC outside of "reasonable business hours"; and (3) a requirement that the border personnel of the contiguous countries be trained in the terms of the agreements.

As mentioned, UAC apprehended by the Border Patrol are brought to a Border Patrol facility where they are processed. In 2008, the agency issued a memorandum entitled "Hold Rooms and Short Term Custody."[27] Since the issuance of this policy, non-governmental organizations (NGOs) have criticized the Border Patrol for failing to fully uphold the provisions in current law and the *Flores Agreement.*[28] Indeed, the DHS Office of Inspector General (OIG) issued a report in 2010 that concluded while CBP was in general compliance with the *Flores Agreement* it needed to make improvements in certain areas with respect to its handling of UAC.

The 2010 OIG report, however, did not address whether OBP was in compliance with the TVPRA. As highlighted above, the TVPRA requires CBP personnel to screen UAC from contiguous countries for severe forms of trafficking in persons *and* for fear of persecution if they are returned to their country of nationality or last habitual residence. At least one NGO that conducted a two-year study on UAC[29] asserted in its report that OBP doesn't adequately do this nor do they have training in place for their Border Patrol agents.[30]

Immigration and Customs Enforcement (ICE)

ICE is responsible for the physical transfer of UAC from CBP to HHS-ORR. Additionally, ICE may apprehend UAC in the interior during immigration enforcement actions. ICE is also responsible for representing the government in removal procedures before EOIR. Unaccompanied alien children who are not subject to TVPRA's special repatriation procedures for certain children from Mexico or Canada (i.e., voluntary departure) may be placed in standard removal proceedings pursuant to INA §240. The TVPRA specifies that UAC in standard removal proceedings also are eligible to be granted voluntary departure under INA §240B at no cost to the child. The TVPRA requires that HHS ensure, to the greatest extent possible, that UAC have access to legal counsel; and statute also permits HHS to appoint independent child advocates for child trafficking victims and other vulnerable unaccompanied alien children.

ICE is also responsible for the physical removal of all foreign nationals, including UAC, who have final orders of removal or who have elected voluntary departure while in removal proceedings. To safeguard the welfare of all UAC, ICE has established policies for repatriating UAC. The policies include:

- returning the UAC only during daylight hours;
- recording the transfer by making sure that the receiving government official or designee signs for custody;
- returning the UAC through a port designated for repatriation;
- providing the UAC the opportunity to communicate with a consular official prior to departure for the home country; and
- preserving the unity of families during removal.[31]

ICE notifies the country of every foreign national being removed from the Unites States.[32] The ability to affect a removal order is dependent on the ability of the U.S. government to secure travel documents for the alien being removed from the country in question.[33] As a result, the United States is dependent on the willingness of foreign governments to accept the return of their nationals. Each country sets documentary requirements for repatriation of their nationals.[34] While some countries allow ICE to use a valid passport to remove an alien (if the alien is in possession of one), other countries require ICE to obtain a travel document specifically for the repatriation.[35] According to one report, the process of obtaining travel documents can become problematic because countries often change their documentary requirements or raise objections to the return of a juvenile.[36]

Once the foreign country has issued travel documents, ICE arranges transport of the UAC and, if flying, accompanies the UAC on the flight to their home country. The majority of ICE's UAC removals are conducted by commercial airlines. ICE provides two escort officers for each UAC.[37] Mexican UAC are repatriated in accordance with Local Repatriation Agreements (LRA), which require notification of the Mexican Consulate for each UAC repatriated. Additional specific requirements apply to each LRA (e.g., specific hours of repatriation).[38]

Office of Refugee Resettlement Program[39]

The Unaccompanied Alien Children Program in ORR/HHS provides for the custody and care of unaccompanied alien minors who have been apprehended by ICE or CBP or referred by other federal agencies. The Trafficking Victims Protection Reauthorization Act (TVPRA) of 2008, which made significant reforms to policies on UAC, directed that HHS ensure that the UAC "be promptly placed in the least restrictive setting that is in the best interest of the child."[40] The HSA requires that ORR develop a plan to ensure the timely appointment of legal counsel for each UAC, ensure that the interests of the child are considered in decisions and actions relating to the care and custody of a UAC, and oversee the infrastructure and personnel of UAC residential facilities, among other responsibilities.[41] ORR also screens the UAC to determine if the child has been a victim of a severe form of trafficking in persons, if there is credible evidence that the minor is at risk should the minor be returned to his or her country of nationality or of last habitual residence, and if the UAC has a possible claim to asylum.

ORR arranges to house the child either in one of its shelters or in a foster care situation; or the UAC program reunites the child with a family member. The *Flores Agreement* outlines the following preference ranking for sponsor types: (1) a parent; (2) a legal guardian; (3) an adult relative; (4) an adult individual or entity designated by the child's parent or legal guardian; (5) a licensed program willing to accept legal custody; or (6) an adult or entity approved by ORR.[42] According to ORR, the majority of the youth are cared for through a network of state-licensed ORR-funded care providers that provide classroom education; mental and medical health services; case management; and socialization and recreation. The state-licensed ORR-funded care providers also facilitate the UAC release to family members or other sponsors who are able to care for them.[43]

In making these placement determinations, ORR conducts a background investigation to ensure the identity of the adult assuming legal guardianship for the UAC and that the adult does not have a record of abusive behavior. ORR may consult with the consulate of the UAC's country of origin as well as interview the UAC to ensure they also agree with the proposed placement. If such background checks reveal evidence of actual or potential abuse or trafficking, ORR may require a home study as an additional precaution.[44] In addition, the parent or guardian is required to complete a Parent Reunification Packet to attest that they agree to take responsibility for the UAC and provide him or her with proper care.[45]

A juvenile may be held in a secure facility only if he or she is charged with criminal or delinquent actions; threatens or commits violence; displays unacceptably disruptive conduct in a shelter; presents an escape risk; is in danger and is detained for their own safety; or is part of an emergency or influx of minors that results in insufficient bed space at non-secure facilities.[46]

Of the children served, ORR reports that ultimately about 85% are reunified with their families.[47] Between FY2008 and FY2010, the length of stay in ORR care averaged 61 days, and total time in custody ranged from less than one day to 710 days.[48] In a May 2014 fact sheet, ORR reported: "The average length of stay in the program is currently near 35 days."[49] It is important to note that removal proceedings continue even when UAC are placed with parents or other relatives.

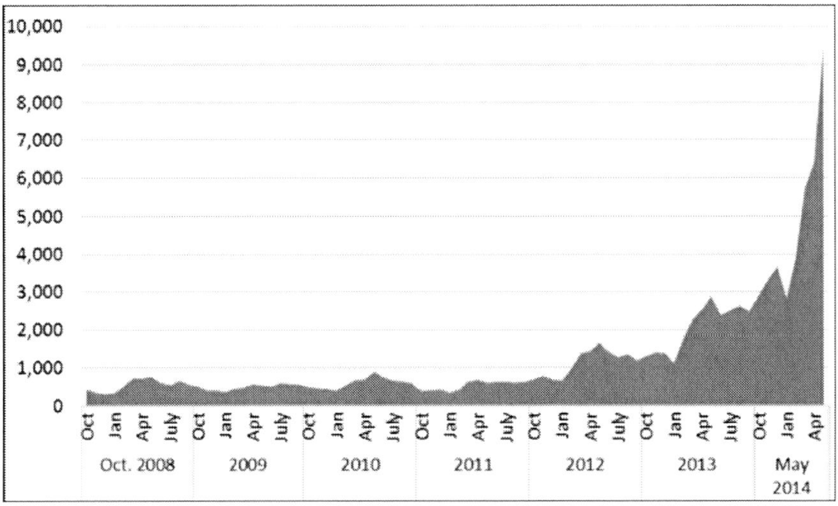

Source: CRS presentation of unpublished data from the Office of Refugee Resettlement.

Figure 2. UACs in ORR Custody, October 2008 through May 2014. (Monthy Referrals).

Figure 2 uses monthly referrals to ORR to illustrate the trends over time and shows a sharp increase in UAC in ORR custody over the past year. Monthly referrals were less than 1,000 until March 2012. By March 2013, monthly referrals to ORR surpassed 2,000 UAC cases, and the number hit 5,527 in March 2014. In May 2014, 9,500 UAC were transferred to ORR. Bear in mind that not all UAC are referred to ORR; for example, some arriving from contiguous countries voluntarily return home.

U.S. Citizenship and Immigration Services

As mentioned, U.S. Citizenship and Immigration Services (USCIS) is responsible for the initial adjudication of asylum applications filed by UAC. If either CBP or ICE find that the child is a UAC and transfer the child to ORR custody, USCIS will generally take jurisdiction over the asylum application, even where there may be some evidence that the child reunited with a parent or legal guardian after CBP or ICE made the UAC determination. In addition, USCIS has initial jurisdiction over asylum applications filed by UACs with pending claims in immigration court, with a case on appeal before the Board of Immigration Appeals, or with a petition for review with a federal court as of the date of enactment of the TVPRA (December 23, 2008). The UAC must appear at any hearings scheduled in immigration court even after he or she has filed for asylum with USCIS.

The Executive Office of Immigration Review

The U.S. Department of Justice Executive Office of Immigration Review (EOIR) is responsible for adjudicating immigration cases, including removal proceedings. Generally, during an immigration removal proceeding, the foreign national and the U.S. government present testimony so that the immigration judge can make a determination on whether the foreign national is removable or qualifies for some type of relief from removal (i.e., the alien is permitted to remain in the United States either permanently or temporarily.)

EOIR has specific policies for conducting the removal hearings of UAC to ensure that UAC understand the nature of the proceedings, can effectively present evidence about their cases, and have appropriate assistance. The policy guidelines discuss possible adjustments to create "an atmosphere in which the child is better able to present a claim and to participate more fully in the proceedings." Under these guidelines, the immigration judges are supposed to:

- establish special dockets for UAC so that they are separated from the general population;
- allow child-friendly courtroom modifications (e.g., judges not wearing robes, allowing the child to have a toy, permitting child to testify from a seat rather than the witness stand, allowing more breaks during the proceedings);
- provide courtroom orientations to familiarize the children with the court;
- explain the proceedings at the outset;
- prepare the child to testify; and
- employ child-sensitive questioning.

Under policy, immigration judges should strongly encourage the use of pro bono legal representation if the child is not represented.

ADMINISTRATIVE AND CONGRESSIONAL ACTION

Both the Administration and Congress have begun to take action to respond to the surge in UAC coming across the border. The Administration has developed a working group to coordinate the efforts of the various agencies involved in responding to the issue. It also has opened additional shelters and holding facilities to accommodate the large number of UAC apprehended at the border. Relatedly, Congress is considering funding increases for HHS/ORR and DHS/CBP.

Administrative Action

The Administration developed a Unified Coordination Group that is comprised of representatives from all of the relevant agencies involved in responding to this issue.[50] Federal Emergency Management Agency (FEMA) Administrator Craig Fugate was named as the Federal Coordinating Official, and will be coordinating the federal response to the UAC issue.[51] Reportedly, the Unified Coordination Group is looking at the large increase in UAC from an incident management perspective. Administrator Fugate's role is to support the lead agencies, CBP and HHS, by bringing in capacity from throughout the federal government so that the lead agencies can focus on their missions.[52]

Reportedly, CBP will maintain primary responsibility for border security operations at and between ports of entry and, working with ICE, provide for the proper care of unaccompanied children when they are temporarily in DHS custody.[53] DHS will continue to coordinate closely with the Departments of Health and Human Services, State, and Defense, the General Services Administration, and other agencies, to ensure a coordinated and fast response within the United States in the short term, and in the longer term to work with the sending countries to undertake reforms to address the causes behind the recent migration trends.[54] DHS is also currently working with the Central American countries on a public education campaign to dissuade UAC from attempting to migrate illegally to the United States.[55]

To deal with the current influx of UAC, HHS/ORR has made use of a network of group homes operated by nonprofit organizations in Texas and other parts of country. These nonprofit organizations have experience providing the types of services that UAC need (e.g., medical, nutritional, educational). In addition, HHS has reached out to the Department of Defense (DOD) for additional assistance in housing UAC. DOD has made facilities available in Lackland Air Force Base in San Antonio, TX, and at Naval Base Ventura County in Oxnard, CA. The Lackland facility can hold 1,200 UAC and had 1,000 UAC as of June 3, 2014. The facility in Ventura can hold 600 UAC and was expected to begin operations on June 6, 2014. According to a press report, these facilities are only supposed to be temporary and are not intended to remain open for more than 120 days.[56]

In addition to the aforementioned efforts, the Corporation for National and Community Service (CNCS), which administers AmeriCorps,[57] and the Department of Justice EOIR have created "Justice AmeriCorps." Justice AmeriCorps is a grant program that will enroll approximately 100 lawyers and paralegals as AmeriCorps members to provide legal representation to UAC during removal proceedings.[58]

On June 20, 2014, the Administration announced additional efforts it is taking to address this issue. In its "Fact Sheet: Unaccompanied Children from Central America," the Administration noted that it has partnered with its Central American counterparts in three key areas: "combating gang violence and strengthening citizen security, spurring economic development, and improving capacity to receive and reintegrate returned families and children." (Security and economic issues are believed to be contributing "push" factors that has led to the massive out migration from Guatemala, Honduras, and El Salvador.) In the fact sheet, the Administration announced assistance it will be providing to Guatemala, Honduras, and/or El Salvador to provide support in the areas of reintegration and repatriation of their citizens, to improve security, to provide economic and educational opportunities and anti-gang and crime prevention programs, and to promote "peace, security, stabilization, and other related rule of law programs."[59] The Administration has collaborated with the other Central American governments on campaigns to inform would-be migrants of the danger of relying on human smuggling networks *and* on reinforcing that recently arriving children will not benefit from current Administrative policies[60] or pending legislation.[61] Thc Administration also announced that it has "enhanced enforcement and removal proceedings."

Congressional Action

In the President's FY2015 budget for the various agencies responsible for the UAC population (i.e., specifically in HHS/ORR and DHS budgets), there wasn't a request for funding increases to help address what has been characterized as a strain on agency resources.[62]

The FY2015 President's budget request for the HHS/ORR program was originally $868 million, which is the same amount that was appropriated in FY2014. However, on May 30, 2014, the Office of Management and Budget updated its cost projections related to the UAC crisis and requested a total of $2.28 billion for FY2015 for the UAC program in the Office of Refugee Resettlement.

The Senate Committee on Appropriations Subcommittee on Labor, Health, and Human Services, and Education and Related Agencies approved the Department of Labor, Health, and Human Services, and Education and Related Agencies FY2015 draft appropriations bill on June 10, 2014. With respect to the UAC program, the subcommittee recommended $1.94 billion, which is $34 million less than the Administration's amended request and a more than $1 billion increase over FY2014 levels. The subcommittee noted the fluidity of the issue and recommended an expansion of HHS transfer authority "to respond to sudden or urgent needs in the future."[63]

For DHS agencies, the Administration's amended request included an additional $166 million for "CBP overtime, contract services for care and support of UAC, and transportation costs."[64] Previously, DHS appropriators criticized the Administration for not requesting additional funding to deal with the crisis;[65] and on June 10, 2014, the House Committee on Appropriations approved the Administration's amended request of $166 million above the budget request.[66]

Policy Challenges

The Administration has recently announced an initiative that is aimed at unifying efforts among the various agencies charged with UAC responsibilities, *and* Congress is considering increasing appropriations for the various agencies involved. These efforts, however, are geared toward responding to the immediate crisis, and there is no way to know whether the numbers of UAC will decrease, increase or level off over the long run. Also, although there is speculation about what is causing the increase in UAC attempting to illegally enter the United States, there is no clear answer to the root causes. A clearer understanding of the factors that make up the "push-pull" of this extraordinary migration will aid the Administration and Congress in framing the most effective policy responses.

In addition, it is unknown how many of these children will qualify for asylum or other forms of immigration relief that may allow them to remain in the United States, or if many of them will be returned to their home countries. If, as some observers have noted, many of the UAC have family in the United States, and many of those family members, in turn, are not legally present, it raises thorny policy questions. Not only does it hinge on what is in the "best interests of the child," it also hinges on what is permissible under the Immigration and Nationality Act and other relevant laws.

End Notes

[1] Senate Judiciary Committee hearing on Oversight of the Department of Homeland Security, June 11, 2014. Hereinafter referred to as Senate oversight hearing.

[2] Guatemala, Honduras, and El Salvador.

[3] Cecilia Muñoz, the White House Director of Domestic Policy Council, "Press Call Regarding the Establishment of the Inter-Agency Unified Coordination Group on Unaccompanied Alien Children," press release, June 3, 2014.

[4] Most commonly these critics cite the Border Security, Economic Opportunity, and Immigration Modernization Act (S. 744), passed by the Senate in 2013, which would allow certain unlawfully present aliens to adjust to a lawful immigration status; and the administrative policy entitled Deferred Action for Childhood Arrivals (DACA), which grants certain aliens who arrived in the United States prior to a certain period as children some protection from removal for at least two years. For an example of these arguments, see U.S. Congress, Senate Committee on the Judiciary, Oversight of the Department of Homeland Security, 113th Cong., 2nd sess., June 11, 2014. For a discussion of S. 744, see CRS Report R43099, Comprehensive Immigration Reform in the 113th Congress: Short Summary of Senate-Passed S. 744, by Ruth Ellen Wasem. For a discussion of DACA, see CRS Report RL33863, Unauthorized Alien Students: Issues and "DREAM Act" Legislation, by Andorra Bruno.

[5] Alien, a technical term appearing throughout the Immigration and Nationality Act (INA), refers to a foreign national who is not a citizen or national of the United States.

[6] The child may have illegally entered the country or been legally admitted but overstayed length of admittance (i.e., a visa overstay.)

[7] 6 U.S.C. §279(g)(2).

[8] A juvenile is defined as an alien under the age of 18. 8 CFR §263.3. In this report, the terms "juvenile," "child," and "minor" are used interchangeably.

[9] A juvenile is classified as unaccompanied if neither a parent nor a legal guardian is with the juvenile alien at the time of apprehension, or within a geographical proximity to quickly provide care for the juvenile. 8 CFR §236.3(b)(1).

[10] White House, Departments of Homeland Security and Health and Human Services, "Press Call Regarding the Establishment of the Inter-Agency Unified Coordination Group on Unaccompanied Alien Children," press release, June 3, 2014.

[11] Over the past three years, there has been an increase in Border Patrol apprehensions of third-country nationals. While the number of those apprehended from Mexico decreased slightly (from 286,154 to 267,734), the number of apprehended third-country nationals increased almost three-fold from 54,098 to 153,055.

[12] William Kandel, Analyst in Immigration Policy, contributed to this section.

[13] The Homeland Security Act of 2002 abolished the Immigration and Naturalization Service (INS) and its functions were split in the Departments of Homeland Security, Justice and Health and Human Services.

[14] Flores v. Meese—Stipulated Settlement Agreement (U.S. District Court, Central District of California, 1997).

[15] See DHS Office of Inspector General, CBP's Handling of Unaccompanied Alien Children, OIG-10-117, Washington, DC, September 2010.

[16] See U.S. Department of Justice, Office of the Inspector General, Unaccompanied Juveniles in INS Custody, Executive Summary, Report no. I-2001-009, September 28, 2001.

[17] ORR assumed care of UAC on March 1, 2003, and created the Division of Unaccompanied Children's Services (DUCS) for addressing the requirements of this population. P.L. 107-296, Section 462.

[18] OBP includes the Border Patrol. OBP and the Border Patrol are used interchangeably throughout this section.

[19] The OFO oversees the CBP Officers who provide inspections of travelers and goods that come through a port of entry.

[20] When both OBP and OFO are referenced in this section, "CBP" is used.

[21] The processing of UAC includes gathering biographic information such as their name and age as well as their citizenship and whether they are unaccompanied. Border Patrol agents also collect biometrics on UAC and query relevant immigration, terrorist, and criminal databases.

[22] The 72-hour time period was established in statute by the TVPRA.

[23] Voluntary departure is a form of discretionary relief that may be offered to certain aliens in lieu of being subject to formal removal proceedings. Aliens accepting an offer of voluntary departure are not inadmissible in the future under INA §212(a)(9). When granted by the border patrol, the procedure is usually referred to as "voluntary return."

[24] P.L. 110-457, §235(a)(2)(A).

[25] 8 U.S.C. §1101 et seq. Although the screening provision only applies to UAC from contiguous countries, in March 2009 DHS issued a policy that, in essence, made the screening provisions applicable to all UAC. U.S. Congress, Senate Committee on the Judiciary, "Trafficking Victims Protection Reauthorization Act: Renewing the Commitment to Victims of Human Trafficking," testimony of Acting Deputy Assistant Secretary Kelly Ryan, September 13, 2011.

[26] In this case, the UAC is permitted to return immediately to Mexico or Canada, and does not face administrative or other penalties. 8 U.S.C. §1225(a)(4).

[27] UAC are held in "hold rooms" at Border Patrol stations. The 2008 memorandum, which is publically available but redacted, outlines agency policy on the care and treatment of individuals in CBP care and custody. See U.S. Customs and Border Patrol, Memorandum on "Hold Rooms and Short Term Custody," June 2, 2008, http://foiarr.cbp.gov/streamingWord.asp?i=378.

[28] See for example, Children at the Border: The Screening, Protection and Repatriation of Unaccompanied Mexican Minors, by Betsy Cavendish and Maru Cortazar, Appleseed, Washington DC, 2011. Hereinafter referred to as Children at the Border.

[29] See Children at the Border.

[30] Relatedly, the 2010 OIG study was unable to determine whether CBP personnel had sufficient training to comply with the provisions in the Flores Agreement. Notably, the Appleseed study (Children at the Border) included site visits to ten Border Patrol facilities as well as site visits to locales in Mexico and interviews with government officials in both countries and minors in custody and who have been repatriated. Whether this limited site visit sample is sufficiently varied to be adequately generalizable to all Border Patrol facilities on the U.S.-Mexico border is unclear.

[31] Email from ICE Congressional Relations, May 16, 2014.

[32] A country clearance is the process by which ICE notifies a foreign country, through the U.S. Embassy abroad, that a foreign national is being repatriated. Additionally, when an alien is being escorted by ICE personnel, the country clearance process is used to notify the U.S. Ambassador abroad that U.S. government employees will be travelling to the country.

[33] Conversation with Doug Henkel, Associate Director, ICE Removal and Management Division, February 20, 2012.

[34] Depending on the country and depending on where the UAC is housed, the consular officers will conduct in-person or phone interviews. Olga Byrne and Elise Miller, The Flow of Unaccompanied Children Through the Immigration System, Vera Institute of Justice, Washington, DC, March 2012, p. 27.

[35] Annex 9 of the Civil Aviation Convention requires that countries issue travel documents, but the convention lacks an enforcement mechanism.

[36] Olga Byrne and Elise Miller, The Flow of Unaccompanied Children Through the Immigration System, Vera Institute of Justice, Washington, DC, March 2012, p. 27.

[37] An additional officer is added for each group that exceeds five UAC. The gender of the officers corresponds to the gender of the children being repatriated. Email from ICE Congressional Relations, May 16, 2014.

[38] Ibid.

[39] William Kandel, Analyst in Immigration Policy, contributed to this section.

[40] §§235(a)-235(d) of TVPRA; 8 U.S.C. §1232(b)(2).

[41] Section 235(c) of the TVPRA and Section 462(b) of the Homeland Security Act of 2002 (HSA, P.L. 107-296) describe conditions for the care and placement of UAC in federal custody.

[42] Flores v. Reno Stipulated Settlement Agreement, 1997, p.10.

[43] Administration for Children and Families, Office of Refugee Resettlement, Unaccompanied Alien Children Program, U.S. Department of Health and Human Services, Fact Sheet, May 2014, http://www.acf.hhs.gov/sites/default/files/orr/ unaccompanied_childrens_services_ fact_sheet.pdf. (Hereinafter ORR UAC Fact Sheet, May 2014.)

[44] Pursuant to the TVPRA of 2008, home studies are required for certain UAC considered especially vulnerable.

[45] Office of Refugee Resettlement, Unaccompanied Children's Services, ORR/DCS Family Reunification Packet for Sponsors (English/Español), http://www.acf.hhs.gov/programs/ orr/resource/unaccompanied-childrensservices#Family%20Reunification%20 Packet%20for%20Sponsors.

46 Center for Human Rights & Constitutional Law, Flores v. Meese: Final Text of Settlement Establishing Minimum Standards and Conditions for Housing and Release of Juveniles in INS Custody, Exhibit 2 (1997).

[47] ORR UAC Fact Sheet, May 2014.
[48] Vera Institute Study, p. 17.
[49] ORR UAC Fact Sheet, May 2014.
[50] Department of Homeland Security, "Statement by Secretary Johnson on Increased Influx of Unaccompanied Immigrant Children at the Border," press release, June 2, 2014, http://www.dhs.gov/news/2014/06/02/statementsecretary-johnson-increased-influx-unaccompanied-immigrant-children-border.
[51] Alejandro Mayorkas, Deputy Secretary of the Department of Homeland Security, "Press Call Regarding the Establishment of the Inter-Agency Unified Coordination Group on Unaccompanied Alien Children," press release, June 3, 2014.
[52] Craig Fugate, Federal Coordinating Administration of the Inter-Agency Unified Coordination Group on UAC, "Press Call Regarding the Establishment of the Inter-Agency Unified Coordination Group on Unaccompanied Alien Children," press release, June 3, 2014.
[53] ICE is also focusing on dismantling the smuggling organizations who are smuggling UAC into the United States.
[54] Department of Homeland Security, "Statement by Secretary Johnson on Increased Influx of Unaccompanied Immigrant Children at the Border," press release, June 2, 2014, http://www.dhs.gov/news/2014/06/02/statementsecretary-johnson-increased-influx-unaccompanied-immigrant-children-border.
[55] Alejandro Mayorkas, Deputy Secretary of the Department of Homeland Security, "Press Call Regarding the Establishment of the Inter-Agency Unified Coordination Group on Unaccompanied Alien Children," press release, June 3, 2014.
[56] Leslie Berestein Rojas, "Emergency Shelter for Unaccompanied Migrant Kids Opening in Ventura County," 89.3 KPCC, Southern California Public Radio, June 5, 2014, http://www.scpr.org/blogs/multiamerican/2014/06/05/16777/ emergency-shelter-for-unaccompanied-migrant-kids-o/.
[57] For more information on the CNCS and AmeriCorps, see CRS Report RL33931, The Corporation for National and Community Service: Overview of Programs and Funding, by Abigail B. Rudman and Benjamin Collins.
[58] Department of Justice and the Corporation for National and Community Service, "Justice Department and CNCS Announce New Partnership to Enhance Immigration Courts and Provide Critical Legal Assistance to Unaccompanied Minors," press release, June 6, 2014, http://www.nationalservice.gov/newsroom/press-releases/2014/justicedepartment-and-cncs-announce-new-partnership-enhance.
[59] The Administration also announced additional funding for ongoing bilateral assistance to the three countries for a variety of programs. "Fact Sheet: Unaccompanied Children from Central America," http://www.whitehouse.gov/thepress-office/2014/06/20/fact-sheet-unaccompanied-children-central-america.
[60] For example, the administrative policy entitled Deferred Action for Childhood Arrivals (DACA) grants certain aliens who arrived in the United States prior to a certain period as children some protection from removal for at least two years.
[61] For example, the Border Security, Economic Opportunity, and Immigration Modernization Act (S. 744) as passed by the Senate would allow certain unlawfully present aliens to adjust to a lawful immigration status.
[62] While the Administration did not request an increase in FY2015 funding for the HHS/ORR UAC program, in its FY2014 budget request the Administration requested a $192 million increase and received an almost $492 million increase over the FY2013 levels.

[63] See Untied States Senate Committee on Appropriations, "FY15 LHHS Subcommittee Markup Bill Summary," June 10, 2014.

[64] Executive Office of the President Office of Management and Budget memo to Representative Nita Lowey, May 30, 2014.

[65] See House Subcommittee on DHS Appropriations markup on April 2, 2014, and House Appropriations Committee markup of the DHS appropriations bill on June 10, 2014.

[66] Previously, the House Subcommittee on DHS Appropriations approved $77 million above the budget request for ICE transportation costs.

In: Unaccompanied Alien Children in the U.S. ISBN: 978-1-63321-832-1
Editor: Paul Snider

Chapter 2

UNACCOMPANIED ALIEN CHILDREN: POTENTIAL FACTORS CONTRIBUTING TO RECENT IMMIGRATION*

William A. Kandel, Andorra Bruno, Peter J. Meyer, Clare Ribando Seelke, Maureen Taft-Morales and Ruth Ellen Wasem

SUMMARY

Since FY2008, the growth in the number of unaccompanied alien children (UAC) from Mexico, El Salvador, Guatemala, and Honduras seeking to enter the United States has increased substantially. Total unaccompanied child apprehensions increased from about 8,000 in FY2008 to 52,000 in the first 8 1/2 months of FY2014. Since 2012, children from El Salvador, Guatemala, and Honduras (Central America's "northern triangle") account for almost all of this increase. Apprehension trends for these three countries are similar and diverge sharply from those for Mexican children. Unaccompanied child migrants' motives for migrating to the United States are often multifaceted and difficult to measure analytically.

---

* This is an edited, reformatted and augmented version of a Congressional Research Service publication R43628, prepared for Members and Committees of Congress, dated July 3, 2014.

Four recent out-migration-related factors distinguishing northern triangle Central American countries are high violent crime rates, poor economic conditions fueled by relatively low economic growth rates, high rates of poverty, and the presence of transnational gangs. In 2012, the homicide rate per 100,000 inhabitants stood at 90.4 in Honduras (the highest in the world), 41.2 in El Salvador, and 39.9 in Guatemala. International Monetary Fund reports show economic growth rates in the northern triangle countries in 2013 ranging from 1.6% to 3.5%, relatively low compared with other Central American countries. About 45% of Salvadorans, 55% of Guatemalans, and 67% of Hondurans live in poverty. Surveys in 2013 indicate that almost half of all unaccompanied children experienced serious harm or threats by organized criminal groups or state actors, and one-fifth experienced domestic abuse.

In 2011, Mexico passed legislation to improve migration management and ensure the rights of migrants transiting the country. According to many migration experts, implementation of the laws has been uneven. Some have questioned whether passage of such legislation has affected in some way the recent flows of unaccompanied children. However, the impact of such laws remains unclear.

Although economic opportunity may motivate some unaccompanied children to migrate to the United States, labor market conditions for low-skilled minority youth have worsened in recent years, even as industrial sectors employing low-skilled workers enjoy improved economic prospects. Educational opportunities may also provide a motivating factor to migration as perceptions of free and safe education may be widespread among the young. Family reunification is reported to be one of the key motives of unaccompanied children. Many have family members among the sizable Salvadoran, Guatemalan, and Honduran foreign-born populations residing in the United States.

While the impacts of actual and perceived U.S. immigration policies have been widely debated, it remains unclear if, and how, specific immigration policies have motivated children to migrate to the United States. Misperceptions about U.S. policies may be a contributing factor. The existence of long-standing humanitarian relief policies confounds causal links between them and the recent surge in unaccompanied children. A notable and recent exception is revised humanitarian relief provisions for unaccompanied children included in the Trafficking Victims Protection Reauthorization Act (TVPRA) of 2008, which affects asylum claims, trafficking victim protections, and eligibility for Special Immigrant Juvenile Status. Some argue that unaccompanied children and their families falsely believe they would be covered under the Deferred Action for Childhood Arrivals (DACA) initiative and legalization provisions in proposed comprehensive immigration reform (CIR) legislation.

INTRODUCTION

In the past several years, and in the past year in particular, the number of unaccompanied alien children (UAC)[1] seeking to enter the United States along the U.S.-Mexico border has surged to unusually high levels. This surge is driven overwhelmingly by migration from El Salvador, Guatemala, and Honduras. Congress has expressed increasing concerns over this situation because of its implications for border security and U.S. immigration policy. Because the surge has occurred recently, and because few sources of data exist to accurately measure the characteristics and motives of these unaccompanied children, immigration observers have advanced a range of explanations for the surge.

The report is not intended to be an exhaustive review of all factors that potentially underlie the recent surge in unaccompanied children. Rather, it discusses major possible contributing factors that have been widely cited in published reports. It also emphasizes factors that may account for the recent surge in unaccompanied children, but not long-standing causes, such as wage and earnings differentials between other countries and the United States. The report distinguishes what are often referred to as "push" and "pull" factors[2] associated with the recent surge. Push factors in this case refer to forces that originate in migrant origin countries which encourage children to emigrate to other countries. Pull factors refer to elements that originate in the United States and encourage children to migrate specifically to this country.

The analytic dichotomy between push and pull factors often blurs in actual circumstances. For example, family reunification may occur after a parent from an origin country secures employment in the United States. Yet, having an employed parent in the United States may easily make a child in an origin country more susceptible to extortion or kidnapping by criminal gangs, which in turn, may motivate the child to migrate to the United States. Hence, having an employed parent in the United States ostensibly acts as a "pull" factor while the threat of violence acts as a "push" factor, but in this example, the latter would not occur without the former.

Migration to another country stems not only from macro-level circumstances such as violence and economic hardship but also personal circumstances and characteristics, such as marital status and risk tolerance. Most children have multiple motives, and how those motives influence their decisions to migrate depend on a range of factors that cannot be measured easily.

This report begins by describing the recent surge in unaccompanied child apprehensions. It discusses several factors widely associated with out-migration from El Salvador, Guatemala, and Honduras, three countries accounting for much of the recent surge of unaccompanied child migrants. These factors include economic conditions and poverty, crime and violence, and conditions related to the migration transit zone between Central America and the United States. The report then discusses three broad factors that may be attracting migrants to the United States: economic and educational opportunity, family reunification, and U.S. immigration policies. It concludes with caveats on the attribution of causes to this situation.

BACKGROUND[3]

Unaccompanied alien children (UAC) are defined in statute as aliens[4] under age 18, who lack lawful immigration status in the United States, and who are without a parent or legal guardian in the United States or lack a parent or legal guardian in the United States who is available to provide care and physical custody.[5] They typically arrive at U.S. ports of entry or are apprehended along the southwestern border with Mexico. Less frequently they are apprehended in the interior and determined to be a juvenile[6] and unaccompanied.[7] Most of these children are aged 14 or older.

The number of unaccompanied children has increased in the past six years and has surged in this current year. In FY2008, the number apprehended by U.S. Customs and Border Protection (CBP) totaled 8,041. In the first 81/2 months of FY2014, apprehensions climbed to 52,000 (*Figure 1*).[8] Nationals of Guatemala, Honduras, El Salvador, and Mexico, have accounted for almost all unaccompanied alien children apprehended at the Mexico-U.S. border during this period.

In the past three years, apprehensions of Mexican unaccompanied children, which rose substantially in FY2009, have since varied between 12,000 and 17,000. In contrast, apprehensions of unaccompanied children from Guatemala, Honduras, and El Salvador have increased considerably during this period. In FY2009, Mexicans accounted for 82% of the 19,668 unaccompanied child apprehensions, while the Central American countries accounted for 17%. By the first eight months of FY2014, the proportions had almost reversed, with Mexican apprehensions comprising only 23% of the 52,000 UAC apprehensions, and UAC from the three Central American countries comprising 75% of the total. The total increase in apprehensions in the past three years stems mainly from large increases in the number of unaccompanied children from the three Central American countries.

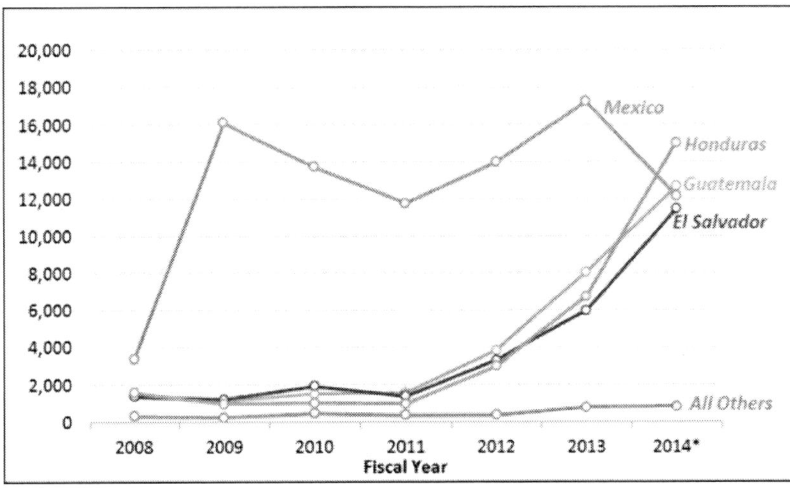

Source: Prepared by Jamie L. Hutchinson, CRS Graphics Specialist. Data from Department of Homeland Security, United States Border Patrol, Juvenile and Adult Apprehensions–Fiscal Year 2013. (Data provided to CRS by request.)

Notes: FY2014 figures are October 1, 2013, to June 15, 2014, representing just over 2/3 of a fiscal year.

Figure 1. UAC Apprehensions by Country of Origin, FY2008-FY2014.

The similarity of the trends characterizing apprehensions of unaccompanied alien children from El Salvador, Guatemala, and Honduras, and their stark divergence from those characterizing unaccompanied Mexican children suggests that factors specific to Central America's "northern triangle"[9] underlies the sudden surge in total unaccompanied child apprehensions. What follows is a discussion of possible causes originating in the countries themselves ("push factors") and other possible causes originating in the United States ("pull factors").

CONDITIONS IN CENTRAL AMERICA AS POSSIBLE "DRIVERS" FOR UNACCOMPANIED CHILD MIGRATION

Central America is a region encompassing seven countries of the isthmus between Mexico and South America: Belize, Costa Rica, El Salvador,

Guatemala, Honduras, Nicaragua, and Panama (*Figure 2).* The overwhelming majority of the unaccompanied child migrants apprehended in Mexico or at the U.S.-Mexico border have come from Guatemala, Honduras, and El Salvador, which are often referred to as the "northern triangle" countries of Central America. High violent crime rates, poor economic conditions fueled by relatively low economic growth rates, relatively high poverty rates, and the presence of transnational gangs appear to be some of the main distinguishing factors between these three northern triangle countries and other countries in the region.[10]

Unaccompanied child migrants' motives for emigrating appear to be multifaceted. In 2013, the U.N. High Commissioner for Refugees (UNHCR) conducted interviews with a representative group of about 400 unaccompanied minors from El Salvador, Guatemala, Honduras, and Mexico, all of whom had arrived in the United States since FY2012.[11] Most of the unaccompanied minors provided multiple reasons for leaving their countries. Many left to reunite with family or pursue opportunities in the United States. Of those interviewed, 21% mentioned joining a family member, 51% mentioned economic opportunity, and 19% mentioned education.[12]

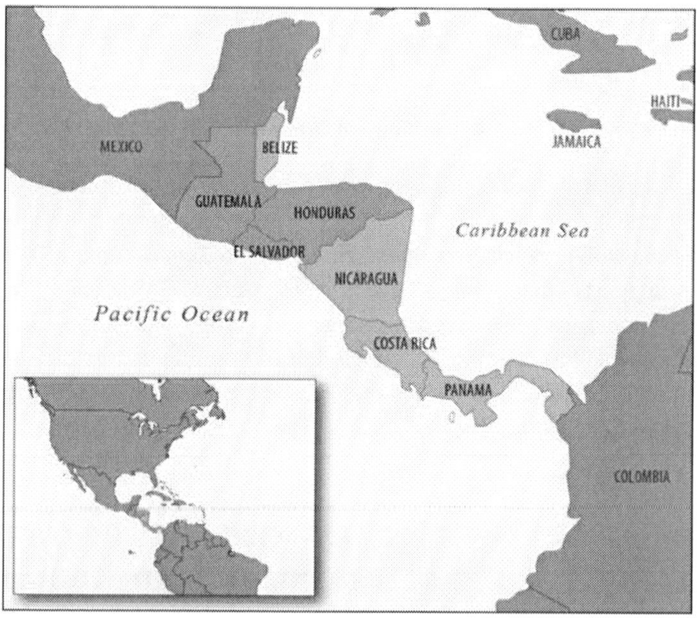

Source: Prepared by Amber Hope Wilhelm, CRS Graphics Specialist.

Figure 2. Map of Central America and Neighboring Countries.

Violence also played a large role in their decisions to emigrate. Nearly half of the children (48%) said they had experienced serious harm or had been threatened by organized criminal groups or state actors, and more than 20% had been subject to domestic abuse. As recently as 2006, only 13% of unaccompanied child migrants from Central America interviewed by UNHCR presented any indication they were fleeing societal violence or domestic abuse.

Endemic poverty also appears to play a role in the emigration of unaccompanied minors, as 16% of those interviewed mentioned economic deprivation as a motive. There is some variation depending on country of origin, with Salvadorans being more likely to cite societal violence and Guatemalans being more likely to cite economic deprivation as motives for emigration (see *Table 1*).[13] Other studies involving interviews with unaccompanied children yield similar results.[14]

Table 1. Primary Reasons Unaccompanied Children Emigrate (Percentage of minors interviewed by UNHCR in 2013 citing each factor)

Country of Origin	Societal Violence	Domestic Abuse	Economic Deprivation or Social Exclusion	Family or Opportunities in the United States	Other
El Salvador	66%	20%	7%	80%	35%
Guatemala	20%	23%	29%	84%	39%
Honduras	44%	24%	21%	82%	34%
Mexico	59%	17%	7%	80%	34%
Total	48%	21%	16%	81%	35%

Source: UNHCR, Children on the Run.

Notes: Sums exceed 100% since the majority of the children interviewed provided multiple reasons for emigrating. Column categories were grouped by source author, and more detailed reasons cannot be provided.

Economic Stagnation and Poverty

El Salvador, Guatemala, and Honduras are each considered lower middle income economies by the World Bank. Per capita gross domestic product (GDP) in 2014 is estimated to be $4,014 in El Salvador, $3,684 in Guatemala, and $2,368 in Honduras.[15] The countries have maintained what are viewed by most economists as generally sound macroeconomic policies in recent years, and enjoyed stable economic growth until the onset of the global financial crisis and U.S. recession in 2009. At that time, the Salvadoran and Honduran economies contracted and the Guatemalan economy slowed significantly, demonstrating how all three countries are vulnerable to external shocks as a result of their open economies[16] and close ties to the United States.[17] Although all three economies have rebounded since 2010, growth rates have yet to fully recover (see *Figure 3*). El Salvador posted an economic growth rate of just 1.6% in 2013, the lowest of any country in Central America.[18]

Economic growth in the region has been inhibited by slow economic growth in major markets (Europe, China, the United States) as well as domestic factors, such as a coffee rust (roya fungus) outbreak, hurricanes and other natural disasters, and weak productivity.[19] The coffee rust epidemic, which in 2013 affected 74% of the coffee crop in El Salvador, 70% of the coffee crop in Guatemala, and 25% of the coffee crop in Honduras, led to nearly 200,000 jobs being lost across the three countries.[20] Employment and wages in the coffee sector have continued to fall over the past year, depriving many poor households of a significant source of income.[21]

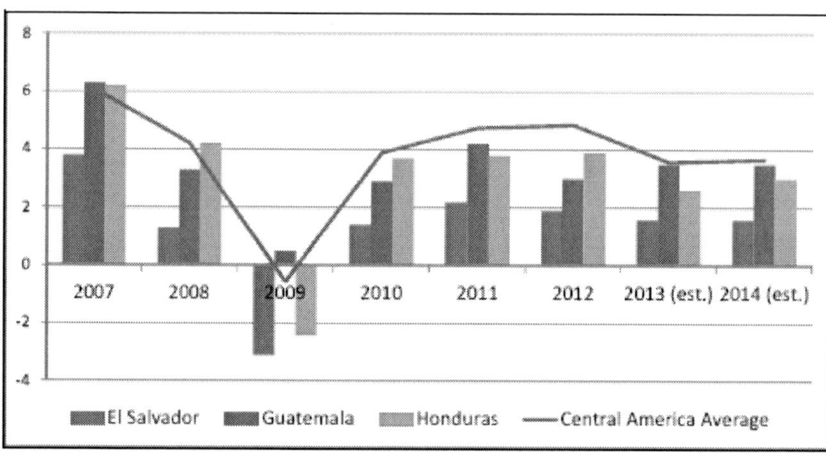

Source: International Monetary Fund (IMF), World Economic Outlook Database, April 2014, accessed June 2014.

Note: Growth rates for 2013 and 2014 are IMF estimates.

Figure 3.Annual Percentage Change in Real Gross Domestic Product (GDP): 2007-2014.

Central American countries are also vulnerable to other types of natural disasters. For example, a tropical storm that hit El Salvador in 2011 caused more than $800 million in damage to roads, infrastructure, and agriculture.[22]

The northern triangle countries also struggle with low productivity rates, particularly when compared to competitors in East Asia. Tariff preferences provided through the Dominican Republic-Central America-United States Free Trade Agreement (CAFTA-DR) appear to be important in keeping apparel producers in those countries competitive in the U.S. market.[23]

Economic growth and slightly higher levels of social investment have led to improved social conditions in the region over the past decade. Nevertheless, poverty remains widespread. According to the U.N. Economic Commission for Latin America and the Caribbean (ECLAC), about 45% of Salvadorans, 55% of Guatemalans, and 67% of Hondurans live in poverty. Guatemala and Honduras have the highest income disparities in Central America, exacerbated by the social exclusion of indigenous people and ethnic minorities.[24] The top 10% of earners account for 47% of national income in Guatemala and 43% of national income in Honduras.[25]

Crime and Violence

El Salvador, Guatemala, and Honduras have long struggled to address high levels of crime and violence, but the deterioration in security conditions has accelerated over the past decade.[26] Counternarcotics efforts in Colombia and Mexico have put pressure on drug traffickers in those countries, leading some to battle over territory in Central America—a region with fewer resources and weaker institutions dedicated to addressing criminal activity.[27] Increasing flows of illicit narcotics have coincided with rising levels of violence and have contributed to the corruption of government officials.

Gangs such as *Mara Salvatrucha* (MS-13) and the "18th Street" gang (M-18) also play a major role in crime and violence in the northern triangle region, but are not significantly present in other Central American countries.[28] The 18th Street gang was formed by Mexican youth in the Rampart section of Los Angeles in the 1960s who were not accepted into existing Hispanic gangs. MS-13 was created during the 1980s by Salvadorans in Los Angeles who had fled the country's civil conflict.[29] Both gangs later expanded their operations to Central America. This process accelerated after the United States began deporting illegal immigrants, many with criminal convictions, back to the northern triangle region after the passage of the Illegal Immigrant Reform and Immigrant Responsibility Act (IIRIRA) of 1996.[30] In general, Central American countries whose migrants did not emigrate to the Los Angeles area, such as Nicaragua or Panama, did not receive large numbers of gang-deportees in the 1990s.[31]

The MS-13 and 18th Street gangs engage in a variety of activities, such as kidnapping, extortion, and forced recruitment, which often have more of an impact on the day-to-day lives of Salvadorans, Guatemalans, and Hondurans than drug-trafficking.[32] On October 11, 2012, the Treasury Department designated the MS-13 as a significant transnational criminal organization whose assets would be targeted for economic sanctions pursuant to Executive Order (E.O.) 13581.[33] State Department officials have estimated that roughly 85,000 members of MS-13 and M-18 reside in the northern triangle countries, with the highest per capita concentration in El Salvador.[34]

Table 2. Estimated Homicide Rates in Central America and Mexico: 2007-2012 (Homicides per 100,000 people)

Country	2007	2008	2009	2010	2011	2012
Belize	33.9	35.1	32.2	41.8	39.2	44.7
Costa Rica	8.3	11.3	11.4	11.3	10.0	8.5
El Salvador	57.1	51.7	70.9	64.1	69.9	41.2
Guatemala	43.4	46.1	46.5	41.6	38.6	39.9
Honduras	50.0	60.8	70.7	81.8	91.4	90.4
Nicaragua	12.8	13.0	14.0	13.5	12.5	11.3
Panama	12.7	18.4	22.6	20.6	20.3	17.2
Mexico	7.8	12.2	17.0	21.8	22.8	21.5

Source: U.N. Office on Drugs and Crime (UNODC), Global Study on Homicide 2013: Trends, Contexts, Data, March 2014, http://www.unodc.org/documents/gsh/pdfs/2014_GLOBAL_HOMICIDE_BOOK_web.pdf.

Note: 2012 is the most recent year for which comparable data are available at this time.

Over the past decade, homicide rates have increased significantly in Honduras and remained at elevated levels in El Salvador and Guatemala. According to the U.N. Office on Drugs and Crime, in 2012 (the most recent year for which comparable data are available), the homicide rate per 100,000 inhabitants stood at 90.4 in Honduras, 41.2 in El Salvador, and 39.9 in Guatemala (see *Table 2).*[35] Although local statistics suggest that homicide rates declined slightly in each of the three countries in 2013, they remain among the highest in the world. Moreover, there are indications that the homicide rate has begun to climb once again in El Salvador as the gang truce that has been in effect since 2012 has unraveled.[36] Other crimes, such as theft and extortion, also remain at elevated levels. In 2012, 29% of Salvadorans,

34% of Guatemalans, and 32% of Hondurans reported that someone in their household had been the victim of some form of crime within the previous 12 months.[37]

Many children also must contend with violence at home. Although domestic abuse—including physical, emotional, and sexual abuse—often goes unreported and undocumented, it is believed to be widespread in the region.[38] According to scholars, Central American cultural norms legitimize the use of violence in interpersonal relationships, including physical discipline of children and violence against women.[39] Studies have found that children who are left behind as a result of one or both parents migrating abroad are more vulnerable to abuse. This is especially true of children whose mothers have migrated.[40]

Unaccompanied Migrant Children: Why Not from the Rest of Central America?

In FY2012, the number of unaccompanied children apprehended at the U.S. border originating from the northern triangle countries ranged from about 3,000 to 4,000 per country. That same year, there were only 4 unaccompanied children from Belize, 5 from Costa Rica, 43 from Nicaragua, and none from Panama.[41]

Many observers speculate that children are not migrating from Belize, Costa Rica, Nicaragua, and Panama because those countries have experienced greater economic growth and/or less crime and violence than the northern triangle countries. In 2013, the International Monetary Fund (IMF) estimated that economic growth rates in the northern triangle countries ranged from 1.6% to 3.5%. Most of the other countries' rates were indeed higher: Belize grew by an estimated 1.6%, Costa Rica grew by an estimated 3.5%, Nicaragua grew by an estimated 4.2%; and Panama grew by an estimated 8%.[42] Per capita gross domestic product (GDP) in three of these four countries is higher than in the northern triangle as well: Belize's per capita GDP is $4,659, Costa Rica's is $10,892, and Panama's is $11,824. About 18% of Costa Rica's population and 25% of Panama's live in poverty, the lowest poverty rates in the isthmus.[43] Although Nicaragua's per capita GDP is lower than all the other Central American countries, at $1,929, and its poverty rate of 58% is closer to that of Guatemala (55%), it has social welfare programs that provide many services to mitigate its poverty to some degree. The Nicaraguan economy has also been expanding in recent years.

Most of these non-northern triangle countries can also be characterized as less violent than their neighbors. Costa Rica, Nicaragua, and Panama have the lowest levels of homicides in Central America (although Belize has the second- highest rate in the region) (see *Table 2*). None of the four countries has the same degree of problems with gangs tied to larger and more organized U.S. gangs that their neighbors have; their gangs are more local.[44]

MIGRATION TRANSIT ZONE CONDITIONS AND MEXICO'S MIGRATION POLICIES

Conditions of migration facing unaccompanied children likely play a considerable role in determining whether they emigrate to the United States. While the persistence of economic stagnation, poverty, and criminal violence may explain why flows of unaccompanied minors have increased, the journey through Central America and Mexico to the United States has become more costly and dangerous. Unauthorized migrants from Central America, often lacking legal protection in Mexico because of their immigration status, have reportedly become increasingly vulnerable to human trafficking, kidnapping, and other abuses.[45] Corrupt Mexican officials have been found to be complicit in activities such as robbery and abuse of authority.[46] While Mexico has stepped up immigration enforcement in some areas (see below), enforcement along train routes frequently used by Central American child migrants continues to be lacking.[47]

As U.S. border security has tightened, more unauthorized Central American migrants have reportedly turned to smugglers (*coyotes*),[48] who in turn must pay money to transnational criminal organizations (TCOs) such as Los Zetas, to lead them through Mexico and across the U.S.- Mexico border.[49] The Administration has estimated that 75-80% of unaccompanied child migrants are now traveling with smugglers.[50] Some smugglers have reportedly sold migrants into situations of forced labor or prostitution (forms of human trafficking) in order to recover their costs; other smugglers' failure to pay Los Zetas has reportedly resulted in massacres of groups of migrants.[51] Mass grave sites where migrants have been executed by TCOs have been recovered in recent years.

The Mexican government appears to be attempting to balance enforcement and humanitarian concerns in its migration policies. Implementation of its new laws and policies has been criticized both by those who favor more enforcement and those who favor more migrants' rights.[52] In addition to stepping up efforts against human trafficking and passing new laws to stiffen penalties for alien smuggling (2010) and human trafficking (2012), Mexico enacted a comprehensive migration reform law in 2011 and secondary legislation to implement that law in 2012. Previously, Mexico's immigration law, the General Population Act (GPA) of 1974, limited legal immigration and restricted the rights of foreigners in Mexico, with unauthorized migrants subject to criminal penalties. In 2008, the Mexican Congress reformed the GPA to decriminalize simple migration offenses, making unauthorized migrants subject to fines and deportation, but no longer subject to imprisonment. In May 2011, it passed a broader reform of the GPA.[53]

Contrary to some media reports, Mexico's 2011 law did not create a transit visa for migrants crossing through Mexico, as civil society groups had been advocating. As a result of the law, Mexico now requires visas for Central Americans entering its territory (aside from those on temporary work permits or those possessing a valid U.S. visa).

According to many migration experts, implementation of Mexico's 2011 migration law has been uneven. While some purges of corrupt staff within the National Migration Institute (INM) in the Interior Ministry have occurred in the past year, implementation of the migration law has been hindered by the government's failure to more fully overhaul INM.[54] Some experts maintain that Mexico lacks the funding and institutions to address traditional migration flows, much less the increasing numbers of U.S.-bound unaccompanied children that its agents are detaining. Mexico has only two shelters for migrant children and no foster care system in which to place those who might be granted asylum.

Despite provisions to improve migrants' rights included in the 2011 migration law, the Mexican government also continues to remove large numbers of Central American adult migrants, arrest smugglers of those migrants, and return unaccompanied child migrants to Central America.[55] According to INM, Mexico detained 86,929 foreigners in 2013, 80,079 of whom were removed (79,416 people were removed in 2012). Of those who were removed, some 97.4% originated in the northern triangle countries of Central America. In the first four months of 2014, Mexico removed some 24,000 people from the northern triangle countries, 9% more than during that period in 2013.[56] Child protection officers from INM accompanied 8,577 children to their countries of origin in 2013 and 6,330 from January through May 2014; 99% of those children originated in northern triangle countries.[57]

With U.S. support, the Mexican government in 2013 started implementing a southern border security plan that has involved the establishment of 12 naval bases on the country's rivers and three security cordons that stretch more than 100 miles north of the Mexico-Guatemala and Mexico-Belize borders.[58]

Factors in the United States Associated with Immigration of Unaccompanied Children

Forces that potentially attract unaccompanied children to the United States may be more subjective than forces that cause them to leave their home countries. Unlike the prevalence of actual violence or deprivation associated with daily economic hardship, for instance, the perception of economic opportunity or the chance to obtain legal authorization to live in the United States may often conflict with what is legally and actually possible. Several reports suggest that migrant smugglers prey on potential migrants' desperation by misleading them with false information about such possibilities.[59]

Immigration observers have made numerous, sometimes conflicting assertions of the importance of one or another pull factor, relying on a range of empirical evidence. Despite considerable public attention, the precise combination of motives driving unaccompanied children to migrate to the United States remains unclear. The discussion below considers three widely cited motivations: economic and educational opportunity, family reunification, and recent U.S. immigration policies.

Economic and Educational Opportunity[60]

Unaccompanied children regularly cite economic opportunity in the United States as a reason for their emigration north.[61] Since almost all are school-aged children, it remains unclear how this stated aspiration should be interpreted. Given endemic poverty in northern triangle countries, slow economic growth, and the large and long-standing income disparity between the triangle countries and the United States, it remains unclear the extent to which fluctuations in economic conditions in the United States actually affect children's migration decisions.

In the United States, current employment levels for minority youth are low relative to all other labor market groups.[62] In the immediate term, the potential for unaccompanied children to participate in the U.S. labor market is constrained in most cases by lack of English language skills, limited educational attainment, and, given their age, the extent to which U.S. laws permit their labor force participation.[63] Assuming they found employment, such constraints would likely relegate them to low-skilled, low-wage sectors of the U.S. economy.

Apart from what unaccompanied children cite as pull factors, U.S. labor market conditions likely affect their parents and relatives residing in the United States, which in turn, may play a critical role in the recent surge. Improving employment prospects, for instance, could more readily provide parents with the means to afford the expense of their children's migration to this country and lead to greater desire for family reunification as discussed below.[64]

At a national level, macroeconomic data on the U.S. economy indicate that despite overall improvement, considerable slack remains in labor markets, with labor force participation remaining weak and the unemployment rate and other measures of labor force utilization remaining well above most estimates of the long-run sustainable rate.[65]

Labor market conditions for low-skilled workers are especially challenging. Bureau of Labor Statistics (BLS) employment data by educational attainment show that employment for workers with less than a high school diploma[66] fell by about 5 million jobs between 2007 and 2014.[67] Thus, despite some indications of economy-wide recovery and U.S. labor market improvement, the demand for low-skill workers has not recovered over the same period that has witnessed the surge of unaccompanied children.

Regarding unauthorized workers, while extensive academic scholarship has analyzed their role, impact, and prospects in the U.S. labor force, government reporting is hindered by data limitations. Government statistics, as a rule, do not capture legal status of the foreign-born workforce. Therefore, assessing how U.S. economic conditions serve as a magnet for typically low-skilled and often unauthorized workers cannot be measured directly and is usually estimated or inferred by assessing the employment outlook of industrial sectors most likely to employ low skilled and unauthorized workers.

Research from the Pew Hispanic Center, which produces authoritative statistics on the unauthorized population, suggests that unauthorized workers concentrate in four low-skilled industrial sectors: farming; building, grounds-keeping and maintenance; construction; and food preparation and serving.[68] With the exception of farming, the BLS projects that these occupations are expected to grow close to or above the average rate of all occupations in the coming decade.[69]

Hence, the economic prospects for low-skilled, low-wage, and typically unauthorized workers appears mixed. While employment in low-skilled sectors of the economy has suffered more and recovered less than that of other sectors in the past seven years since the economic downturn, the employment prospects for the economic sectors most likely to employ such workers appears on par with or above the national average. Nonetheless, perceptions of opportunities may have greater impact than fluctuations in U.S. economic and labor market conditions.

Unaccompanied children also cite educational opportunity in the United States as a reason for their emigration north.[70] Unauthorized aliens in the United States are able to receive free public education through high school. In 1982, the Supreme Court's decision in Plyler v. Doe prohibited states from restricting access of children to public elementary and secondary education on the basis of immigration status.

The Court's ruling did not concern access to higher education, however, and both the federal government and some states have adopted measures that limit unlawfully present aliens' eligibility for admission to public institutions of higher education, in-state tuition, or financial aid.[71]

Family Reunification

Family reunification is often cited as a primary reason for the recent large-scale migration of unaccompanied children to the United States.[72] Surveyed unaccompanied children cite family reunification as one of the main reasons for migrating to the United States.[73] The desire to reunite with family stems from family separation that occurs when one or both parents migrate to a destination country for more remunerative employment. Prior to the mid-1990s, migrants from Mexico and Central America who worked in the United States often returned regularly to be with their families in their origin countries.[74] Increased border enforcement in the mid-1990s gradually made unauthorized entry into the United States more difficult and expensive, which had the unintended consequence of creating a "caging effect" by encouraging unauthorized aliens to settle permanently in the United States rather than working temporarily and regularly returning home.[75]

Demographic and survey data provide evidence of sizable linkages between the three countries dominating the recent spike in unaccompanied child apprehensions and their foreign-born populations living in the United States. In 2012, the foreign-born populations from El Salvador (1,254,501), Guatemala (880,869), and Honduras (535,725) ranked as the 6th, 10th, and 16th largest groups, respectively, of all foreign born groups.[76] From the perspective of the source country, U.N. survey data indicate that sizable percentages of children residing in these three countries have at least one parent living in the United States.[77] Were data available on other relatives living in the United States, such as siblings or extended relatives, these percentages would be higher.

The desire for family reunification is also driven by the perception that children who are not immediately returned to their home countries can reside with their family members for periods extending several years, as discussed below under "*U.S. Immigration Policies.*" Upon apprehension, unaccompanied children are immediately given a *Notice to Appear* (NTA) before an immigration judge who will adjudicate their case to remain in the United States.[78] Receipt of an NTA indicates the start of immigration proceedings.

Yet, by law, persons apprehended by Customs and Border Patrol (CBP) and whom CBP determines to be unaccompanied children from countries other than Mexico and Canada, must be turned over to the care and custody of Health and Human Services (HHS), Office of Refugee Resettlement (ORR) while they await their removal hearing.[79] Unaccompanied children are moved from the custody of the law enforcement agency that apprehended them to a human services agency experienced with child welfare and family reunification. ORR is required to place these children in the least restrictive setting possible that accounts for the child's best interests.[80] In an estimated 90% of these cases, children are placed with parents, siblings, and extended relatives who currently reside in the United States.[81]

The Immigration and Nationality Act (INA) contains provisions allowing foreign nationals to reside lawfully in the United States if they are sponsored by parents and siblings who are U.S. citizens or Lawful Permanent Residents.[82] However, sizable proportions of these family members are estimated to be unauthorized aliens.[83] According to DHS, the estimated unauthorized populations in 2012 of Salvadorans, Guatemalans, and Hondurans living in the United States was 690,000, 560,000, and 360,000, respectively, representing 55%, 64%, and 67% of all foreign-born residents from those three countries living in the United States.[84]

The length of time unaccompanied children can expect to wait until their removal hearing may play a role for incentivizing their migration to the United

States. As of March 2014, the average wait time nationwide for all immigration proceedings was 19 months.[85] However, the length of time until a final judgment occurs varies widely depending on appeals and individual circumstances.[86] Surges in caseloads, such as that caused by the current influx of unaccompanied children, can also tax the limited resources of the immigration court system, further extending wait times for removal hearings, and possibly fostering a perception among foreign nationals that a unique opportunity exists to exploit this administrative backlog. Rumors of these backlogs and the potential for being reunited with family—even if temporarily—reportedly have reached emigrant-sending communities in Central America.[87]

U.S. Immigration Policies

The possible relationship between U.S. immigration policies (actual policies as well as perceptions of policies) and the surge in arrivals of unaccompanied children has been the subject of heated discussion among immigration observers and policy makers. It is not known if, and how, specific immigration policies may have influenced decisions to try to enter the United States unlawfully. News reports, however, suggest that perceptions of unspecified U.S. policies toward alien minors may have played a role. According to a June 2014 *New York Times* article:

> [C]hildren, parents, immigration officials, lawyers and activists interviewed say that there has been a subtle shift in the way the United States treats minors.
>
> That perception has inspired parents who have not seen their children for years to hire so-called coyotes, guides often associated with organized crime, to bring them north. It has prompted other parents to make the trip with toddlers in tow, something rarely seen before in the region.[88]

Similarly, a June 2014 article by the Migration Policy Institute makes reference to "some evidence of a growing perception among Central Americans that the U.S. government's treatment of minors, as well as minors traveling in family units, has softened in recent years."[89] As discussed below, there have been recent changes in the treatment of unaccompanied children who arrive in the United States, in accordance with the Trafficking Victims Protection Reauthorization Act of 2008.

Much of the debate about the possible role of U.S. immigration policy in the surge has focused on specific policies and proposals that some may believe can offer unaccompanied children the prospect of a period of stay in the United States or U.S. lawful permanent resident status. A March 2014 *Miami Herald* article, after noting that many arriving children are fleeing gang violence, stated:

> But children are also being sent by families who believe they could qualify for immigration reform—if Congress ever acts on it—or for President Barack Obama's 2012 Deferred Action for Childhood Arrivals program known as DACA.[90]

For its part, the Obama Administration maintains that the driving force behind the surge "is what's happening in [the unaccompanied children's] home countries."[91] The Administration has stated, however, that misinformation about U.S. policies has been a contributing factor. White House Domestic Policy Council Director Cecilia Muñoz, as reported by Bloomberg News in June 2014, blamed the increase in unaccompanied children attempting to cross the border in part on 'misinformation' about immigration law and administration actions regarding minors that "is being deliberately promulgated by criminal networks' involved in smuggling aliens into the U.S."[92] Other observers who reject the argument that Administration policies are responsible for the surge in unaccompanied child arrivals point to "Obama's aggressive deportation policy since ... 2009."[93]

U.S. immigration policies and proposals – both legislative and administrative – that have been widely cited as possible factors in the surge or that are relevant to the treatment of unaccompanied children who arrive in the United States are discussed here.

Humanitarian Forms of Immigration Relief

As discussed above, child migrants report that they are fleeing violence, deprivation, abuse, or other hardships in their home countries as well as reuniting with family already in the United States. At issue is whether U.S. immigration policies that provide humanitarian relief to those who are fleeing such situations may serve as a magnet to foreign nationals. These humanitarian policies include asylum, relief for trafficking victims, and special immigrant status for juveniles.[94]

As these policies on humanitarian relief have been in place for many years, it is difficult to make a causal link between them and the recent surge in unaccompanied children from Central America. The only notable and recent revisions to the policies on humanitarian relief for unaccompanied children were included in the Trafficking Victims Protection Reauthorization Act (TVPRA) of 2008, as discussed below.

Asylum

Many immigration observers expect that a large proportion of unaccompanied children seeking immigration relief in the United States will apply for asylum. The United States has long held to the principle that it will not return a foreign national to a country where his or her life or freedom would be threatened. This principle is embodied in several provisions of the INA, most notably in provisions defining refugees and asylees that the Refugee Act of 1980 added to the INA.[95]

In 2008, the TVPRA revised the procedures and policies for those unaccompanied children who file for asylum, most notably requiring that unaccompanied children from contiguous countries (i.e., Canada and Mexico) be screened for possible asylum claims. Subsequently, DHS opted to screen all unaccompanied children for possible asylum claims.[96] In addition, the TVPRA gives U.S. Citizenship and Immigration Services (USCIS) asylum officers "initial jurisdiction over any asylum application filed by" an unaccompanied child.[97]

To receive asylum, foreign nationals must demonstrate a well-founded fear that if returned home, they will be persecuted based upon one of five characteristics: race, religion, nationality, membership in a particular social group, or political opinion. Because "fear" is a subjective state of mind, assessing the merits of an asylum case rests in large part on the credibility of the claim and the likelihood that persecution would occur if the alien is returned home.

Asylum claims for the current surge of unaccompanied children may be complicated by uncertainty as to whether their circumstances meet the criteria established by the INA for asylum seekers. It remains to be seen the extent to which this legal option would offer immigration relief to the many unaccompanied children who claim asylum on the basis of feared persecution due to gang-related violence.[98] Data on the percentage of unaccompanied alien children who receive asylum is not available.[99]

Trafficking Victims

Unaccompanied children who arrive at the U.S. border may have valid claims for immigration relief on the basis of being trafficking victims.[100]

Foreign nationals who are victims of severe forms of trafficking are eligible for T nonimmigrant status and ultimately lawful permanent residence if they meet certain conditions.[101] U.S. statute defines severe forms of trafficking to mean: (A) sex trafficking in which a commercial sex act is induced by force, fraud, or coercion, or in which the person induced to perform such act has not attained 18 years of age; or (B) the recruitment, harboring, transportation, provision or obtaining of a person for labor or services, through the use of force, fraud, or coercion for the purpose of subjection to involuntary servitude, peonage, debt bondage, or slavery.[102]

In addition to requiring that unaccompanied children from contiguous countries be screened for possible asylum claims, the TVPRA of 2008 requires that they be screened to determine that the unaccompanied child has not been a victim of a severe form of trafficking in persons.

In March 2009, DHS issued a policy that essentially made the trafficking screening provisions applicable to all unaccompanied children.[103] Immigration judges generally issue a relatively small number of T "visas" (856 in FY2013), and the number of unaccompanied alien children among these is unknown.

Special Immigrant Juveniles

More than two decades ago, Congress created an avenue for unauthorized children who become dependents of the court to become lawful permanent residents (LPRs).[104] Any child or youth who was born in a foreign country; who lives without legal authorization in the United States; who has experienced abuse, neglect, or abandonment; and who meets other specified eligibility criteria may be eligible for the LPR classification of special immigrant juvenile (SIJ).

Among other things, TVPRA of 2008 amended the SIJ eligibility provisions to 1) remove the requirement that a juvenile court deem a juvenile eligible for long-term foster care and 2) replace it with a requirement that the juvenile court find reunification with one or both parents not viable. According to USCIS legal guidance, an eligible SIJ would include the following:

> [An unauthorized child] who has been declared dependent on a juvenile court; whom a juvenile court has legally committed to, or placed under the custody of, an agency or department of a State; or who has been placed under the custody of an individual or entity appointed by a State or juvenile court. Accordingly, petitions that include juvenile court orders legally committing a juvenile to or placing a juvenile under the custody of an individual or entity appointed by a juvenile court are now eligible.[105]

SIJ status is one of the few forms of immigration relief in the INA that specifically takes into account the best interests of the child. By statute, ORR must consent to any court having jurisdiction to determine the custody status or placement of a juvenile alien in ORR custody for SIJ status.[106] It is not known how many unaccompanied children have ultimately obtained SIJ status.[107]

Deferred Action for Childhood Arrivals (DACA) and Legalization Proposals

Some observers have singled out the Obama Administration's Deferred Action for Childhood Arrivals (DACA) initiative and legalization provisions in proposed comprehensive immigration reform (CIR) legislation as possible factors in the surge of unaccompanied child arrivals. The DACA initiative provides temporary protection from removal to certain individuals who were brought to the United States before age 16 and meet other criteria. Among the criteria is continuous residence in the United States since June 15, 2007.[108] Although new arrivals would not be eligible for DACA, some argue that unaccompanied children and their families falsely believe that they would be covered.[109]

CIR legislation introduced in Congress in recent years typically has included provisions to enable certain unauthorized aliens to become lawful permanent residents of the United States. In 2013, the Senate passed a CIR bill (the Border Security, Economic Opportunity, and Immigration Modernization Act; S. 744) that would establish a general legalization program for unauthorized aliens who have been continuously physical present in the United States since December 31, 2011, and meet other criteria; dependent spouses and children of principal applicants would have to have maintained continuous physical presence in the United States since December 31, 2012, and meet other requirements. S. 744 would provide a special pathway to LPR status for successful applicants under the general legalization program who entered the United States before age 16 and satisfy other requirements.[110] Newly arriving unaccompanied children would not be eligible for the S. 744 legalization programs.

CONCLUSION

This report has conceptualized possible factors contributing to the recent and sizable increase in unaccompanied children into "push" and "pull" forces.

The former comprise conventional and long-standing forces such as endemic poverty and lack of economic opportunity, as well as recent causes, such as the rise of gangs and drug trafficking organizations that have destabilized El Salvador, Guatemala, and Honduras and severely limited these countries' ability to protect their youth. The latter include more subjective factors, such as aspirations for employment and education, the desire to reunite with family members, and perceptions related to U.S. immigration policies.

With information relatively scare, and circumstances changing rapidly, it becomes challenging to accurately measure or gauge which factors are the most important drivers of the current surge. For example, surveys by organizations with distinct goals may sometimes yield findings that place substantially more emphasis on one factor over another. Absent full scale representative information, it may be difficult to draw conclusions about the magnitude of any single factor or its relative strength over another. As noted above, the division between push and pull factors blurs as multiple factors affect individuals making personal decisions to migrate.

End Notes

[1] In this report, we refer to unaccompanied alien children as unaccompanied children.

[2] The terms "push factor" and "pull factor" have long been used in demographic research to explain human migration.

[3] For information on unaccompanied alien children, see CRS Report R43599, Unaccompanied Alien Children: An Overview, by Lisa Seghetti, Alison Siskin, and Ruth Ellen Wasem.

[4] Alien, a technical term appearing throughout the Immigration and Nationality Act (INA), refers to a foreign national who is not a citizen or national of the United States. This report uses "unaccompanied alien children" and "unaccompanied children" interchangeably.

[5] 6 U.S.C. §279(g)(2).

[6] A juvenile is defined as an alien under the age of 18. 8 C.F.R. §263.3. In this report, the terms "juvenile," "child," and "minor" are used interchangeably.

[7] A juvenile is classified as unaccompanied if neither a parent nor a legal guardian is with the juvenile alien at the time of apprehension, or within a geographical proximity to quickly provide care for the juvenile. 8 C.F.R. §236.3(b)(1).

[8] If extrapolated at the same rate to the end of the fiscal year, the figure would reach roughly 73,000. News reports have cited an internal DHS memorandum estimating that FY2014 apprehensions could total 90,000. Alicia A. Caldwell, Associated Press, "Border Patrol resources stretched thin as children illegally enter U.S. alone," PBS Newshour, The Rundown, June 5, 2014.

[9] This term is often used to refer to these three countries as a group.

[10] For more information, see CRS Report R41731, Central America Regional Security Initiative: Background and Policy Issues for Congress, by Peter J. Meyer and Clare Ribando Seelke.

[11] U.N. High Commissioner for Refugees (UNHCR), Children on the Run: Unaccompanied Children Leaving Central America and Mexico and the Need for International Protection, March 12, 2014, http://www.unhcrwashington.org/ sites/default/files/1_UAC_Children%20on%20the%20Run_Full%20Report.pdf, (hereinafter referred to as "UNHCR, Children on the Run"). Children interviewed were part of the increase in unaccompanied children beginning in FY2012. Almost all were interviewed while in the custody of the Office of Refugee Resettlement, the agency within the U.S. Department of Health and Human Services to which they are referred after apprehension. Children were identified by a random selection process that accounted for age, nationality, sex, and date of U.S. arrival. For more on the study's methodology, see pp. 18-22. Caution must be used in generalizing a single study to the entire population of unaccompanied children.

[12] Ibid.

[13] Ibid.

[14] See, for example, Women's Refugee Commission, Forced from Home: The Lost Boys and Girls of Central America, October 2012; and Elizabeth G. Kennedy, "'No Place for Children': Central America's Youth Exodus," InSight Crime, June 23, 2014.

[15] International Monetary Fund (IMF), World Economic Outlook Database, April 2014, accessed June 2014.

[16] An open economy is an economy with relatively few barriers to trade or investment (as opposed to a closed or protectionist economy). Open economies are more integrated into the international market than closed economies, and thus more vulnerable to external shocks.

[17] Close ties means the countries are heavily reliant on exports to the United States, remittances from the United States, and investment from the United States.

[18] IMF, World Economic Outlook Database, April 2014, accessed June 2014.

[19] Economist Intelligence Unit, Country Reports on El Salvador, Guatemala, and Honduras, June 2014.

[20] The coffee rust epidemic is also a problem in the rest of Central America but Costa Rica, Panama, and to a certain extent, Nicaragua can handle such economic and natural disaster shocks more effectively because of their comparatively well developed economies, lower levels of poverty, and/or stronger social safety nets.

[21] International Coffee Organization, Report on the Outbreak of Coffee Leaf Rust in Central America and Action Plan to Combat the Pest, May 13, 2013, p. 3; Famine Early Warning Systems Network (FEWS NET), Coffee Producer and Laborer Income to Decline for a Second Consecutive Year, Special Report: Central America, February 2014, http://www.fews.net/sites/default/files/documents/reports/FEWS%20NET%20coffee%20rust%20shock%20report%20update_2014_02_en_0.pdf.

[22] U.N. Office for the Coordination of Humanitarian Affairs, "Revision of the Flash Appeal for El Salvador 2011," press release, December 7, 2011.

[23] If apparel produced in Asian countries gains duty-free access to the U.S. market through the proposed Trans-Pacific Partnership agreement (TPP), it could displace apparel manufactured with U.S. fabric in Central America, causing job losses in those industries. CRS Report R42694, The Trans-Pacific Partnership (TPP) Negotiations and Issues for Congress, coordinated by Ian F. Fergusson; and CRS Report R42772, U.S. Textile Manufacturing and the Trans-Pacific Partnership Negotiations, by Michaela D. Platzer.

[24] Poverty rates are 17.8% in Costa Rica, 25.3% in Panama, and 58.3% in Nicaragua. Figures for Belize are unavailable. U.N. Economic Commission for Latin America and the Caribbean (ECLAC), Social Panorama of Latin America 2013, p. 50.

[25] U.N. Economic Commission for Latin America and the Caribbean (ECLAC), Statistical Yearbook for Latin America and the Caribbean, 2013, December 2013.

[26] For more information, see CRS Report R41731, Central America Regional Security Initiative: Background and Policy Issues for Congress, by Peter J. Meyer and Clare Ribando Seelke.

[27] Michael Shifter, "Central America's Security Predicament," Current History, February 1, 2011

[28] For background, see CRS Report RL34112, Gangs in Central America, by Clare Ribando Seelke.

[29] For the history and evolution of these gangs, see Tom Diaz, No Boundaries: Transnational Latino Gangs and American Law Enforcement, Ann Arbor, M.I.: University of Michigan Press, 2009

[30] IIRIRA expanded the categories of noncitizens subject to deportation and made it more difficult for foreign nationals to get relief from removal.

[31] Ana Arana, "How the Street Gangs Took Central America," Foreign Affairs, May/June 2005.

[32] Of the unaccompanied minors interviewed by UNHCR, 27% reported that they had been harmed or threatened by gangs. This includes nearly 62% of the Salvadorans. UNHCR, 2014, op. cit.

[33] The criteria established for declaring a transnational criminal organization pursuant to Executive Order 13581 are available at http://www.whitehouse.gov/the-press-office/2011/07/25/executive-order-blocking-property-transnationalcriminal-organizations. U.S. Department of the Treasury, "Treasury Sanctions Latin American Criminal Organization," press release, October 11, 2012.

[34] U.S. Department of State, "Gangs, Youth, and Drugs – Breaking the Cycle of Violence," Remarks by William R. Brownfield, Assistant Secretary, Bureau of International Narcotics and Law Enforcement Affairs, at the Institute of the Americas, press release, October 1, 2012. In 2012, the U.N. Office on Drugs and Crime (UNODC) estimated total MS-13 and M-18 membership in Guatemala, El Salvador, and Honduras at a more modest 54,000. UNODC, Transnational Organized Crime in Central America and the Caribbean: a Threat Assessment, September 2012.

[35] By comparison, the rates for Belize, Costa Rica, Nicaragua, and Panama were 45, 9, 11 and 17. UNODC, Global Study on Homicide 2013: Trends, Contexts, Data, March 2014, http://www.unodc.org/documents/gsh/pdfs/ 2014_GLOBAL_HOMICIDE_BOOK_web.pdf.

[36] CRS Report R43616, El Salvador: Background and U.S. Relations, by Clare Ribando Seelke; Carlos Martínez and José Luis Sanz, "Gobierno Desmantela la Tregua y los Homicidios Alcanzan 30 en un Día," El Faro, May 24, 2014.

[37] By comparison, the figures for Belize, Costa Rica, Nicaragua, and Panama were 15%, 34%, 25%, and 11%, respectively. Mitchell A. Seligson, Amy Erica Smith, and Elizabeth J. Zechmeister, eds., The Political Culture of Democracy in the Americas, 2012: Towards Equality of Opportunity, LAPOP, January 25, 2013, p. 144.

[38] Isabel Aguilar Umaña and Jeanne Rikkers, Nine Strategies to Prevent Youth Violence in Central America, Interpeace, April 2012, p.9.

[39] World Bank, Crime and Violence in Central America, September 2010, p. 54.

[40] Caroline Bakker, Martina Elings-Pels, and Michele Reis, The Impact of Migration on Children in the Caribbean, U.N. Children's Fund (UNICEF), Paper No. 4, August 2009, p. 8.

[41] U.S. Border Patrol, "Unaccompanied Children (Age 0-17) Apprehensions, FY2008 through FY2012," February 4, 2013.

[42] U.N. Economic Commission for Latin America and the Caribbean (ECLAC), Social Panorama of Latin America 2013, p. 50. (In this section, Belize is not listed if data for it were unavailable.)

[43] ECLAC, Social Panorama of Latin America 2013, p.17.

[44] See CRS Report RL34112, Gangs in Central America, by Clare Ribando Seelke, pp. 3-4.

[45] Steven Dudley, Transnational Crime in Mexico and Central America: Its Evolution and Role in International Migration, Woodrow Wilson International Center for Scholars & Migration Policy Institute, November 2012, http://www.wilsoncenter.org/sites/default/files/ transnational_crime_mexico_centralamerica.pdf.

[46] Adam Isacson, Maureen Meyer, and Gabriela Morales, Mexico's Other Border: Security, Migration, and the Humanitarian Crisis as the Line with Central America, Washington Office on Latin America (WOLA), June 2014, available at http://www.wola.org/news/ new_wola_report_mexicos_other_border (hereinafter referred to as WOLA, Mexico's Other Border Security.)

[47] Ibid.

[48] Human smuggling typically involves the provision of a service, generally procurement or transport, to people who knowingly consent to that service in order to gain illegal entry into a foreign country. For more information, see CRS Report RL34317, Trafficking in Persons: U.S. Policy and Issues for Congress, by Alison Siskin and Liana Rosen.

[49] See Caitlin Dickson, "How Mexico's Cartels are Behind the Border Kid Crisis," The Daily Beast, June 23, 2014.

[50] White House, Office of the Vice President, "Remarks to the Press with Q&A by Vice President Joe Biden in Guatemala," press release, June 20, 2014.

[51] Oscar Martinez, "How the Zetas Tamed Central America's 'Coyotes,'" Insight Crime, May 1, 2014.

[52] WOLA, Mexico's Other Border Security.

[53] Mexico's 2011 migration reform was aimed at (1) guaranteeing the rights and protection of all migrants in Mexico; (2) simplifying Mexican immigration law in order to facilitate legal immigration; (3) establishing the principles of family reunification and humanitarian protection as key elements of the country's immigration policy; and (4) concentrating immigration enforcement authority within the National Migration Institute (INM) in the Interior Ministry in order to improve migration management and reduce abuses of migrants by police and other officials. For a general description of the law in English, see Gobierno Federal de México, "Mexico's New Law on Migration," September 2011, available at http://usmex.ucsd.edu/assets/028/12460.pdf.

[54] Reforms that migration experts have recommended include raising hiring standards for immigration agents, regulating how migrants should be treated, and strengthening internal and external controls over migration agents. Sonja Wolf et. al., Assessment of the National Migration Institute: Towards an Accountability System for Migrant Rights in Mexico, INSYDE, 2014.

[55] From January through May 2014, the Mexican government arrested 431 people for breaking provisions in the migration law; most of those individuals were accused of smuggling-related crimes. Gobierno de Mexico, Sistema Institucional de Información Estadística (SIIE), "Incidencia Delictiva del Fuero Federal, 2014."

[56] Gobierno de Mexico, Secretaría de Gobernación, Instituto Nacional de Migración, Boletín de Estadística Migratorias, 2013. 2014 statistics are available at http://www. politicamigratoria.gob.mx/.

[57] Gobierno de Mexico, Secretaría de Gobernación, Instituto Nacional de Migración, "Reintegra INM a Más de 14 Mil Niños Migrantes con sus Familias," Boletín 31/14, June 11, 2014.

[58] The State Department has provided $6.6 million of mobile Non-Intrusive Inspection Equipment (NIIE) and approximately $3.5 million in mobile kiosks, operated by Mexico's National Migration Institute, that capture the biometric and biographic data of individuals transiting southern Mexico. Total State Department support is likely to reach at least $86.6 million. The U.S. Department of Defense (DOD) has also provided training to troops patrolling the border, communications equipment, and support for the development of Mexico's air mobility and surveillance capabilities. WOLA, op. cit. U.S. Department of State, Bureau of International Narcotics and Law Enforcement Affairs, "INL Assistance for Mexico's Southern Border Strategy," fact sheet, June 2014. For background, see CRS Report R41349, U.S.-Mexican Security Cooperation: The Mérida Initiative and Beyond, by Clare Ribando Seelke and Kristin Finklea.

[59] The White House, Office of the Vice President, "Readout of the Vice President's Meetings on Unaccompanied Minors and Immigration Reform," press release, June 26, 2014; and "Under-age and on the move: A wave of unaccompanied children swamps the debate over immigration," The Economist, June 28, 2014.

[60] Craig Elwell, Specialist in Macroeconomic Policy, Government and Finance Division, and Michael Garcia, Attorney in the American Law Division, both contributed to this section.

[61] UNHCR, Children on the Run.

[62] CRS Report R42519, Youth and the Labor Force: Background and Trends, by Adrienne L. Fernandes-Alcantara.

[63] The Fair Labor Standards Act (FLSA) sets 14 years of age as the minimum age for employment, and limits the number of hours worked by minors under the age of 16. Unauthorized minors who file affirmatively for asylum may apply for work authorization after six months. For more information on asylum, see CRS Report RL32621, U.S. Immigration Policy on Asylum Seekers, by Ruth Ellen Wasem.

[64] Smuggling an unauthorized migrant from Central America can cost as much as $10,000. See United Nations Office on Drugs and Crime, Smuggling of migrants: the harsh search for a better life, 2014, http://www.unodc.org/toc/en/ crimes/migrant-smuggling.html, accessed by CRS on June 27, 2014; and Bryan Roberts, Gordon Hanson, and Derekh Cornwell, et al., An Analysis of Migrant Smuggling Costs along the Southwest Border, Department of Homeland Security, Office of Immigration Statistics, Working Paper, November 2010.

[65] CRS Report R43476, Returning to Full Employment: What Do the Indicators Tell Us?, by Marc Labonte.

[66] Half of all Central American foreign-born adults living in the United States lacked a high school diploma in 2010. See CRS Report R41592, The U.S. Foreign-Born Population: Trends and Selected Characteristics, by William A. Kandel, p. 18.

[67] U.S. Department of Labor, Bureau of Labor Statistics, Current Population Survey, Table A-4, available at http://www.bls.gov/webapps/legacy/cpsatab4.htm.

[68] These four sectors accounted for an estimated 73% of all unauthorized worker employment. Pew Hispanic Center, A Portrait of Unauthorized Immigrants in the United States, by Jeffrey S. Passel, and D'Vera Cohn, April 14, 2009.

[69] U.S. Department of Labor, Bureau of Labor Statistics, Employment Projections: 2012-2022 Summary, December 19, 2013, http://www.bls.gov/news.release/ecopro.nr0.htm, accessed June 27, 2014.

[70] UNHCR, Children on the Run.

71 For more information, see CRS Report RL33863, Unauthorized Alien Students: Issues and "DREAM Act" Legislation, by Andorra Bruno; and "Noncitizens and Eligibility for HEA Federal Student Aid Programs" in CRS Report R43302, Postsecondary Education Issues in the 113th Congress, coordinated by David P. Smole.

72 See for instance, Muzaffar Chishti and Faye Hipsman, "Dramatic Surge in the Arrival of Unaccompanied Children Has Deep Roots and No Simple Solutions," Migration Information Source, June 13, 2014; and "Under-age and on the move: A wave of unaccompanied children swamps the debate over immigration," The Economist, June 28, 2014.

73 UNHCR, Children on the Run.

74 Such migration patterns are fairly universal. See for example, "When Mothers and Fathers Migrate North: Caretakers, Children, and Child Rearing in Guatemala", by Michelle J. Moran-Taylor, in Latin American Perspectives, (Vol. 35, No. 4, July, 2008), pp. 79-95; for a broader treatment, see Douglas S. Massey, "World in Patterns and Processes of International Migration in the 21st Century," Paper prepared for Conference on African Migration in Comparative Perspective, Johannesburg, South Africa, June 4, 2003.

75 CRS Report R42138, Border Security: Immigration Enforcement Between Ports of Entry, by Lisa Seghetti. For more on how U.S. immigration policy affected migration flows, see Wayne Cornelius, "Evaluating Recent US Immigration Control Policy: What Mexican Migrants Can Tell Us," in Crossing and Controlling Borders: Immigration Policies and Their Impact on Migrants' Journeys, ed. Mechthild Baumann, Astrid Lorenz, and Kerstin Rosenhow (Farmington, MI: Budrich Unipress Ltd, 2011); Douglas S. Massey, Jorge Durand, and Nolan J. Malone, Beyond Smoke and Mirrors: Mexican Immigration in an Era of Economic Integration (Russell Sage Foundation, 2002).

76 Other Central American countries ranked considerably lower: Nicaraguans were 31st, Panamanians were 55th, Costa Rican were 67th, and Belizians were 86th. Mexicans represent the largest foreign-born population residing in the United States. For El Salvador, the population residing in the United States is one fifth the size of population living in El Salvador (6.3 million). Source: 2012 American Community Survey (ACS) Public Use Micro Sample (PUMS).

77 The figure is 49% in El Salvador, 27% in Guatemala and 47% in Honduras. By comparison, the figure for Mexico is 22%. Source: UNHCR, Children on the Run.

78 For more information on the processing of unaccompanied alien children, see CRS Report R43599, Unaccompanied Alien Children: An Overview, by Lisa Seghetti, Alison Siskin, and Ruth Ellen Wasem.

79 The Homeland Security Act of 2002 (HSA; P.L. 107-296) divided responsibilities for the processing and treatment of UAC between the newly created Department of Homeland Security (DHS) and the Department of Health and Human Services' (HHS) Office of Refugee Resettlement (ORR). The Trafficking Victims Protection Reauthorization Act of 2008 (P.L. 110-457, Section 235) differentiated treatment according to whether or not unaccompanied children originated from the contiguous countries of Mexico and Canada. Unaccompanied alien children from Mexico and Canada may also be turned over to HHS-ORR if they are determined to be victims or potential victims of trafficking, if they claim asylum, or if they do not consent to return voluntarily.

80 The TVPRA directed HHS to ensure that unaccompanied children "be promptly placed in the least restrictive setting that is in the best interest of the child." §§235(a)-235(d) of TVPRA; 8 U.S.C. §1232(b)(2). See also "What is the "best interest of the child" standard, and how does it apply to immigration detention and removal decisions?" in CRS Report R43623,

Unaccompanied Alien Children—Legal Issues: Answers to Frequently Asked Questions, by Kate M. Manuel and Michael John Garcia.

[81] Administration for Children and Families, Office of Refugee Resettlement, Unaccompanied Alien Children Program, U.S. Department of Health and Human Services, Fact Sheet, May 2014.

[82] See CRS Report R43145, U.S. Family-Based Immigration Policy, by William A. Kandel.

[83] As a policy, ORR does not inquire as to the legal status of the family member with whom the unaccompanied child is placed.

[84] Bryan Baker and Nancy Rytina, Estimates of the Unauthorized Immigrant Population Residing in the United States: January 2012, Department of Homeland Security, Office of Immigration Statistics, March 2013. For comparison, the unauthorized proportion of the total foreign-born population for Mexico is 58%. These figures do not account for considerable numbers of U.S.-born children whose parents were born in these countries. For more on the demographics of legal status among the foreign-born, see CRS Report R41592, The U.S. Foreign-Born Population: Trends and Selected Characteristics, by William A. Kandel.

[85] This figure is based upon an analysis by the Transactional Records Access Clearinghouse (TRAC) of data obtained from the U.S. Department of Justice's Executive Office for Immigration Review (EOIR) for all immigration cases, not just those involving unaccompanied children. See TRAC Immigration data, http://trac.syr.edu/ phptools/ immigration/ court_backlog, accessed June 2014.

[86] The 19 month figure is an average for all immigration courts, and comprises a range of periods, some of which extend far beyond 19 months.

[87] Jennifer Scholtes, "CBP Chief: Policies may be Fueling Spike in Minors Crossing Border Illegally," CQ Roll Call, April 2, 2014; Julia Preston, "Hoping for Asylum, Migrants Strain U.S. Border," New York Times, April 10, 2014; David Nakamura, "Influx of Minors across Texas Border Driven by Belief They will be Allowed to Stay in U.S.," Washington Post, June 13, 2014.

[88] Frances Robles, "Wave of Minors on Their Own Rush to Cross Southwest Border," New York Times, June 4, 2014, (hereinafter cited as Robles, New York Times).

[89] Muzaffar Chishti and Faye Hipsman, "Dramatic Surge in the Arrival of Unaccompanied Children Has Deep Roots and No Simple Solutions," Migration Information Source, June 13, 2014, http://www.migrationpolicy.org/article/ dramatic-surge-arrival-unaccompanied-children-has-deep-roots-and-no-simple-solutions.

[90] Chardy, Alfonso, "Number of Unaccompanied Minors Arriving Illegally in U.S. Is Rising," Miami Herald, March 29, 2014. Newly arriving children would not, in fact, benefit from DACA or the Senate-passed comprehensive immigration reform bill (S. 744) in the 113th Congress.

[91] Quoted in Robles, New York Times, op.cit.

[92] Dorning, Mike, "Obama Boosts Border Security as Unaccompanied Minors Rise," Bloomberg News, June 20, 2014.

[93] Richard Cowen, "Waves of Immigrant Minors Present Crisis for Obama, Congress," Reuters.com, May 28, 2014.

[94] Another possible form of relief, Temporary Protective Status (TPS), is not discussed in this report because it currently does not apply to unaccompanied children arriving from the northern triangle. For information on TPS, see CRS Report RS20844, Temporary Protected Status: Current Immigration Policy and Issues, by Ruth Ellen Wasem and Karma Ester.

[95] CRS Report R41753, Asylum and "Credible Fear" Issues in U.S. Immigration Policy , by Ruth Ellen Wasem.

[96] 8 U.S.C. §1101 et seq. Within 48 hours DHS personnel must screen the unaccompanied child to determine that he or she has not been a victim of a severe form of trafficking in persons and that there is no credible evidence that the minor is at risk should the minor be returned to his country of nationality or of last habitual residence; that the unaccompanied child does not have a possible claim to asylum; and that the unaccompanied child is able to make an independent decision to voluntarily return to his country of nationality or of last habitual residence.

[97] §§235(a) – 235(d) of TVPRA; 8 U.S.C. §1232. Prior to the TVPRA revisions, the unaccompanied children who sought asylum did so during a removal proceeding before an immigration judge in the Department of Justice's (DOJ) Executive Office for Immigration Review (EOIR). USCIS guidelines require that the asylum officer conduct "child-appropriate interviews taking into account age, stage of language development, background, and level of sophistication." The guidelines also note that the child's age may affect the analysis of his or her asylum status (e.g., in considering whether the harm the child suffered amounts to persecution, in evaluating the child's possibly limited knowledge of events, etc.). Where a child is unable to identify all relevant motives for the persecution, the guidelines state that "a nexus can still be found if the objective circumstances support the child's claim that the persecutor targeted the child based on one of the protected grounds. If the Asylum Officer decides that an unaccompanied children in removal proceedings is not eligible for a grant of asylum, case processing will depend on the status of the unaccompanied child's case before EOIR. The Asylum Office coordinates with Immigration and Customs Enforcement (ICE) for the transfer of the files of the unaccompanied children not granted asylum back to ICE. Joseph E. Langlois, "Updated Procedures for Minor Principal Applicant Claims, Including Changes to RAPS," Interoffice Memorandum, USCIS Refugee, Asylum, and International Operations Directorate, August 14, 2007, p. 6-7; and Joseph E. Langlois, " Implementation of Statutory Change Providing USCIS with Initial Jurisdiction over Asylum Applications Filed by Unaccompanied Alien Children," Interoffice Memorandum, March 29, 2009.

[98] See "Can UACs obtain asylum due to gang violence in their home countries?" in CRS Report R43623, Unaccompanied Alien Children—Legal Issues: Answers to Frequently Asked Questions, by Kate M. Manuel and Michael John Garcia.

[99] Discussion with Executive Office of Immigration Review (EOIR), Legislative and Public Affairs, June 4, 2014.

[100] For more information on the difference between human trafficking, which involves forms of involuntary coercion, and human smuggling, which involves knowing consent, see CRS Report RL34317, Trafficking in Persons: U.S. Policy and Issues for Congress, by Alison Siskin and Liana Rosen.

[101] To qualify for the "T" visa, the victim of trafficking must also be: physically present in the United States, American Samoa, the Commonwealth of the Northern Mariana Islands, or a U.S. port of entry because of such trafficking, or to participate in investigative or judicial processes associated with such trafficking; have complied with any reasonable request for assistance to law enforcement in the investigation or prosecution of acts of trafficking unless unable to do so due to physical or psychological trauma, or be under the age of 18; and be likely to suffer extreme hardship involving unusual and severe harm upon removal. CRS Report RL34317, Trafficking in Persons: U.S. Policy and Issues for Congress, by Alison Siskin and Liana Rosen.

[102] §103(8) of P.L. 106-386; 22 U.S.C. 7102.

[103] U.S. Congress, Senate Committee on the Judiciary, "Trafficking Victims Protection Reauthorization Act: Renewing the Commitment to Victims of Human Trafficking," testimony of DHS Acting Deputy Assistant Secretary Kelly Ryan, September 13, 2011.

[104] The provision was initially aimed at children of unauthorized aliens who had been abused, neglected or abandoned.

[105] Letter from Donald Neufeld, Acting Associate Director, Domestic Operations, and Pearl Chang, Acting Chief, Office of Policy, to USCIS Field Leadership, March 9, 2009, http://www.uscis.gov/sites/default/files/USCIS/Laws/ Memoranda/Static_Files_Memoranda/2009/TVPRA_SIJ.pdf.

[106] INA 101(b)(27)(J)(iii)(I).

[107] CRS Report RL34500, Unauthorized Aliens' Access to Federal Benefits: Policy and Issues, by Ruth Ellen Wasem, pp. 6-7.

[108] See CRS Report RL33863, Unauthorized Alien Students: Issues and "DREAM Act" Legislation, by Andorra Bruno.

[109] Muzaffar Chishti and Faye Hipsman, "Dramatic Surge in the Arrival of Unaccompanied Children Has Deep Roots and No Simple Solutions," Migration Information Source, June 13, 2014.

[110] See CRS Report R43097, Comprehensive Immigration Reform in the 113th Congress: Major Provisions in Senate-Passed S. 744, by Ruth Ellen Wasem.

In: Unaccompanied Alien Children in the U.S. ISBN: 978-1-63321-832-1
Editor: Paul Snider

Chapter 3

UNACCOMPANIED ALIEN CHILDREN— LEGAL ISSUES: ANSWERS TO FREQUENTLY ASKED QUESTIONS*

Kate M. Manuel
and Michael John Garcia

SUMMARY

Recent reports about the increasing number of alien minors apprehended at the U.S. border without a parent or legal guardian have prompted numerous questions about so-called unaccompanied alien children (UACs). Some of these questions pertain to the numbers of children involved, their reasons for coming to the United States, and current and potential responses of the federal government and other entities to their arrival. Other questions concern the interpretation and interplay of various federal statutes and regulations, administrative and judicial decisions, and settlement agreements pertaining to alien minors. This report addresses the latter questions, providing general and relatively brief answers to 14 frequently asked questions regarding UACs.

Some of the questions and answers in the report provide basic definitions and background information relevant to discussions of UACs, such as the legal definition of *unaccompanied alien child*; the difference

---

* This is an edited, reformatted and augmented version of a Congressional Research Service publication R43623, prepared for Members and Committees of Congress, dated June 27, 2014.

between being a UAC and having Special Immigrant Juvenile (SIJ) status; the terms and enforcement of the *Flores* settlement agreement; and why UACs encountered at a port of entry—as some recent arrivals have been—are not turned away on the grounds that they are inadmissible. Other questions and answers explore which federal agencies have primary responsibility for maintaining custody of alien children without immigration status; removal proceedings against such children; the release of alien minors from federal custody; the "best interest of the child" standard; and whether UACs could obtain asylum due to gang violence in their home countries. Yet other questions and answers address whether UACs have a right to counsel at the government's expense; their ability under the Vienna Convention on Consular Relations to have consular officials of their home country notified of their detention; and whether UACs are eligible for inclusion in the Obama Administration's Deferred Action for Childhood Arrivals (DACA) initiative.

Recent reports about the increasing number of alien minors apprehended at the U.S. border without a parent or legal guardian have prompted numerous questions about so- called unaccompanied alien children (UACs).[1] Some of these questions pertain to the numbers of children involved, their reasons for coming to the United States, and current and potential responses of the federal government and other entities to their arrival. Other questions concern the interpretation and interplay of various federal statutes and regulations, administrative and judicial decisions, and settlement agreements pertaining to alien minors.

This report addresses the latter questions, providing general and relatively brief answers to 14 frequently asked questions regarding UACs. The report begins with questions and answers that give basic definitions and background information pertaining to UACs, including how federal law defines *unaccompanied alien child* and the difference between being a UAC and having Special Immigrant Juvenile (SIJ) status. It then turns to questions and answers pertaining to custody, control, and enforcement of immigration laws as to UACs, such as federal agencies' responsibilities in maintaining custody of UACs, and UACs' eligibility for relief from removal. It concludes with questions and answers regarding UACs' rights, privileges, and benefits while in the United States, including whether UACs have a right to counsel at the government's expense in removal proceedings and whether UACs are eligible for inclusion in the Obama Administration's Deferred Action for Childhood Arrivals (DACA) initiative.

Definitions and Background

What Is an Unaccompanied Alien Child?

Pursuant to Section 462 of the Homeland Security Act of 2002, as amended, an *unaccompanied alien child*, is defined as a person who is

- under the age of 18;
- lacks lawful immigration status; and
- either (1) has no parent or legal guardian in the United States or (2) has no parent or legal guardian in the country who is available to provide care and physical custody of the child.[2]

Accordingly, not every minor without lawful immigration status is a UAC. Notably, if a child and parent (or other closely related adult) without lawful immigration status are apprehended by immigration authorities and detained together while awaiting removal, the child is not considered a UAC.[3] Moreover, the fact that a child is initially a UAC does not mean that he/she will remain within the scope of this definition thereafter (e.g., the child is reunited with a parent, or turns 18).

What Is the Difference between Being a UAC and Having Special Immigrant Juvenile (SIJ) Status?

Some—but not necessarily all—UACs may be eligible for Special Immigrant Juvenile (SIJ) status. As previously noted (see "What is an unaccompanied alien child?"), the term *unaccompanied alien child* is broadly defined to include aliens under the age of 18 who have no parent or legal guardian in the United States, or whose parent or legal guardian is unavailable to provide care and physical custody. Eligibility for SIJ status under Section 101(a)(27)(J) of the Immigration and Nationality Act (INA) and its implementing regulations is also limited to aliens who are young (under 21 years of age) and essentially lack the care or custody of their parents or legal guardians.[4]

However, eligibility for SIJ status is further restricted in that a state juvenile court must have determined that the alien is dependent upon the court and eligible for long-term foster care because "family reunification is no longer a viable option" due to abuse, neglect, abandonment, or "a similar basis found under State law."[5] The alien must also have been the subject of administrative or judicial proceedings authorized or recognized by the juvenile court in which it is determined that it would not be "in the alien's best interest to be returned to the alien's or parent's previous country of nationality or ... last habitual residence."[6] Provided these conditions are met, and the alien continues to be dependent upon the juvenile court and eligible for long-term foster care,[7] the alien may petition the Department of Homeland Security (DHS) for SIJ status.[8]

SIJ status, in itself, gives aliens a legal basis to remain in the United States and adjust their status to that of lawful permanent resident aliens (LPRs), which, in turn, would eventually enable them to apply for U.S. citizenship. Specifically, Section 245 of the INA provides that aliens granted SIJ status are deemed to have been paroled—a term discussed in greater detail below at "Why aren't UACs encountered at ports of entry turned away as inadmissible?"—into the United States and may apply for LPR status.[9] Being classified as a UAC, in contrast, does not, in itself, furnish any legal basis to remain in the United States or to adjust to LPR status, although an individual UAC could potentially be able to do so on other grounds discussed below. See "Are children without immigration status eligible for relief from removal?" and "Can UACs obtain asylum due to gang violence in their home countries?".

What is the *Flores* Settlement Agreement?

The *Flores* settlement agreement (also known as the *Flores* agreement or *Flores* settlement) is a 1997 agreement resolving a long-running challenge to certain practices of the then-Immigration and Naturalization Service (INS) as to the detention of UACs.[10] The *Flores* litigation began in 1984, when INS's Western Regional Office adopted a policy that generally barred the release of detained minors to anyone other than a parent or lawful guardian except in "unusual and extraordinary cases."[11] This policy was challenged in a class action lawsuit brought on behalf of detained unaccompanied minors. Following several lower court decisions, the litigation reached the Supreme Court, which rejected a facial challenge to the constitutionality of this policy in its 1993 decision in *Flores v. Reno*. In so doing, a majority of the Court expressly rejected the argument that UACs who have no available parent or guardian have a "fundamental right" to be placed in the custody of a willing and able private custodian, instead of government custody.[12] However, notwithstanding the Court's decision, the *Flores* litigation continued, in part, over the conditions in which UACs were detained, and the parties ultimately concluded that settlement was "in their best interests and best serves the interests of justice."[13]

The *Flores* agreement articulates a number of broad principles and policies applicable to the detention of alien minors, some of which are also reflected in subsequent legislation or regulations. See "Which federal agencies have primary responsibility for maintaining custody of alien children without immigration status?" and "May children without immigration status be released from DHS or HHS custody?". Among other things, the agreement establishes that alien minors in federal custody will be treated with "dignity, respect and special concern for their particular vulnerability as minors."[14] It also establishes procedures for the temporary placement of alien minors following their arrest, which include "expeditiously process[ing]" the minor, providing the minor with a notice of rights, and generally segregating UACs from unrelated adults.[15] In addition, it sets forth a "general policy" favoring the release of UACs "without unnecessary delay" to their parents, legal guardians, adult relatives, certain other adults or entities designated by the parent or guardian, licensed programs willing to accept legal custody, or under certain conditions, another entity or adult individual, in this order of preference.[16]

What the *Flores* agreement may require as to any specific alien is less clear, in part, because the agreement incorporates a number of exceptions to its requirements. For example, the agreement specifically contemplates that the "general policy favoring release" would not preclude the continued detention of individual minors in order to secure their timely appearance before immigration authorities or the immigration court, or to ensure the safety of the minor or other persons.[17] In addition, courts have imposed certain limitations upon the agreement's enforceability.[18] In particular, the agreement has been found to be enforceable only through actions seeking compliance with its terms,[19] not through actions seeking monetary damages for alleged violations of its terms. In particular, at least one court has expressly rejected the argument that the *Flores* agreement "create[s] a due process entitlement (a protected property or liberty interest) because the terms and conditions of the agreement currently serve as interim federal regulations, and the language of the agreement is mandatory with regard to the services and protections to be provided to unaccompanied minors."[20]

Also, where legislation enacted subsequent to the *Flores* agreement provides for alternate treatment of UACs, that legislation governs instead of the agreement.[21]

The *Flores* agreement was entered into in 1997, and was initially set to terminate (except for the requirement that minors generally be housed in licensed facilities) at the earlier of (1) five years after its final approval by the court, or (2) three years after the court determines that federal officials are in substantial compliance with the agreement.[22] However, a 2001 stipulation and order extended its term until "45 days after the federal government promulgates final regulations implementing the Agreement."[23] No such regulations have been promulgated to date.

Why Aren't Uacs Encountered at Ports of Entry Turned Away As Inadmissible?

UACs encountered at ports of entry—as some in the recent surge have been—are generally inadmissible under Section 212(a)(7) of the INA.[24] This section generally bars the admission to the United States of

> any immigrant [who] at the time of application for admission ... is not in possession of a valid unexpired immigrant visa, reentry permit, border crossing identification card, or other valid entry document required by this Act, and a valid unexpired passport, or other suitable travel document, or document of identity and nationality if such document is required under the regulations issued by the [Secretary of Homeland Security].[25]

However, admission is not the same as entry for purposes of the INA. *Admission* is defined as the "lawful entry into the United States after inspection and authorization by an immigration officer."[26] *Entry*, in contrast, is generally seen to encompass any "coming of an alien into the United States,"[27] and may be permitted, pursuant to other provisions of federal law, in circumstances where admission is not legally permissible.

In the case of UACs, Section 235 of the William Wilberforce Trafficking Victims Protection Reauthorization Act (TVPRA) of 2008, as amended, could be said to implicitly authorize UACs to enter the United States.[28] Section 235 distinguishes between UACs from "contiguous countries"—namely, Canada and Mexico—and UACs from other countries. UACs from contiguous countries found at a land border or port of entry who are determined to be inadmissible (e.g., for lack of proper documentation) may be permitted to withdraw their application for admission and be returned to their home country, subject to certain conditions.[29] UACs from other countries, in contrast, are not subject to such treatment, but are instead required to be transferred to the custody of the Secretary of Health and Human Services within 72 hours of being determined to be UACs,[30] as discussed below (see "Which federal agencies have primary responsibility for maintaining custody of alien children without immigration status?").

Other provisions of law could also be construed to permit UACs to enter the United States. Key among these provisions is Section 212(d)(5)(A) of the INA, which permits the Secretary of Homeland Security to *parole*—or permit the physical entry of aliens into the United States without being admitted—on a "case-by-case basis for urgent humanitarian reasons or significant public benefit."[31] Among other things, parole under Section 212(d)(5)(A) is used to permit aliens seeking asylum to enter the United States. See "Can UACs obtain asylum due to gang violence in their home countries?".[32]

CUSTODY, CONTROL, AND ENFORCEMENT

Which Federal Agencies Have Primary Responsibility for Maintaining Custody of Alien Children without Immigration Status?

The primary federal agencies responsible for maintaining custody over alien children without immigration status are DHS and the Department of Health and Human Services (HHS). Many UACs encountered by DHS in the course of its immigration enforcement activities are required to be transferred to HHS custody. However, not all UACs encountered by DHS are required to be transferred to HHS. Notably, HHS does not play a role in detaining certain arriving UACs from contiguous countries (i.e., Canada and Mexico) who have agreed to be voluntarily repatriated to their home countries. Moreover, DHS maintains responsibility over *accompanied* alien children who are detained pending removal.

DHS is the primary agency responsible for enforcing the nation's immigration laws, including by apprehending aliens who attempt to enter the United States without legal authorization, and detecting aliens within the country whose unauthorized presence or commission of a status violation makes them removable.[33] In particular, alien children traveling across a land border or a port of entry may be encountered by immigration enforcement officers within DHS[34]—primarily those within U.S. Customs and Border Protection (CBP).[35] If such children are suspected of attempting to enter or have entered the United States without legal authorization, they may be taken into custody and thereafter removed or otherwise repatriated in accordance with applicable federal immigration statutes and regulations.

Section 462 of the Homeland Security Act of 2002 generally transferred responsibility for the care of UACs (but not accompanied alien children) from immigration enforcement authorities to HHS's Office of Refugee Resettlement (ORR).[36] Once such children are transferred to its custody, ORR is responsible for "coordinating and implementing the care and placement" of the children,[37] including by placing UACs in state-licensed care facilities and foster care.[38] However, the transfer of a UAC from DHS custody to ORR does not preclude DHS from removing the alien from the United States.[39] If a UAC in ORR custody is ultimately ordered removed, DHS may briefly take physical custody of the UAC in order to effectuate his or her removal.[40]

Not every UAC encountered by DHS is required to be transferred to the custody of HHS's ORR.[41] If a UAC from Canada or Mexico is apprehended at a land border or a U.S. port of entry and deemed inadmissible under federal immigration laws, the UAC may be offered the opportunity to be voluntarily returned to his or her home country in lieu of being placed in immigration removal proceedings (a process distinct from "voluntary departure," discussed *infra,* "May children without immigration status be placed in removal proceedings?").[42] If the UAC agrees to repatriation, he/she may generally remain in DHS custody for the brief period until being repatriated.[43]

By statute,[44] a determination must be made within 48 hours that an alien child is eligible for voluntary return on account of being a UAC from Canada or Mexico. If a determination cannot be made within this period, or the child does not meet the criteria for repatriation, DHS must immediately transfer the child to ORR custody.

More generally, other than in exceptional circumstances, any child in the custody of DHS or another federal agency must be transferred to the custody of ORR within 72 hours of the agency having made the determination that he/she is a UAC.[45]

May Children without Immigration Status Be Placed in Removal Proceedings?

Children without immigration status may be placed in removal proceedings.[46] However, federal law requires that UACs (but not other alien children identified for removal) be placed in specific types of proceedings if federal immigration authorities seek to remove them from the United States. Moreover, as discussed earlier ("Which federal agencies have primary responsibility for maintaining custody of alien children without immigration status?"), arriving UACs from Canada and Mexico may be voluntarily returned to their home countries in lieu of being placed in removal proceedings, if certain criteria are met.

Federal statute establishes specific requirements concerning the removal of UACs (but not accompanied children). Many aliens arriving in the United States who are deemed inadmissible by an immigration officer may be immediately ordered removed, through a streamlined process known as expedited removal, which entails a determination of inadmissibility by immigration officials, rather than an immigration judge.[47] However, arriving UACs are exempted from this process.[48] In general, if DHS seeks to remove a UAC from the United States, regardless of whether the UAC is arriving or encountered in the United States, it must place the child in removal proceedings before an immigration judge (sometimes referred to as formal removal proceedings).[49] UACs placed in formal removal proceedings are also required to be provided access to counsel, to the extent practicable and consistent with statutory restrictions on the provision of counsel at the government's expense in immigration proceedings.[50] A UAC is also eligible for voluntary departure under Section 240B of the INA in lieu of undergoing removal proceedings, at no cost to the child.[51]

Special rules govern the handling of arriving UACs from Canada and Mexico. In general, arriving aliens are considered "applicants for admission" into the United States for immigration purposes.[52] As previously discussed (see "Which federal agencies have primary responsibility for maintaining custody of alien children without immigration status?"), arriving UACs who are nationals or habitual residents of Canada and Mexico may be voluntarily returned to their home countries in lieu of being placed in removal proceedings, if they consent to the withdrawal of their application for admission.[53] "Voluntary return" following a withdrawal of an application of admission is a distinct alternative to "voluntary departure" under Section 240B of the INA.[54]

The availability of voluntary return to an arriving UAC from Canada or Mexico is contingent upon immigration authorities determining that the child (1) was not a victim of a "severe form of trafficking" or at risk of being trafficked if repatriated;[55] (2) does not have a fear of repatriation on account of a "credible fear" of persecution; and (3) is able to make an independent decision to agree to repatriation in lieu of being placed in removal proceedings.[56]

Arriving UACs from Canada or Mexico who do not satisfy these criteria, or who do not agree to withdraw their application for admission, may be treated in the same manner as other UACs, including being placed in formal removal proceedings before an immigration judge.[57]

Are Children without Immigration Status Eligible for Relief from Removal?

In certain instances, aliens whose entry or continued presence in the United States is otherwise not permitted under federal immigration law may be eligible for relief from removal.[58] If such relief is granted, an otherwise removable alien may be permitted to remain in the United States and, depending upon the form of relief granted, adjust to LPR status.

There is no statute or treaty-based form of relief available for alien children based solely upon their juvenile status. However, some children without immigration status may obtain relief from removal depending upon their individual circumstances, including whether they are victims of trafficking, would face persecution on a protected ground if returned to their home country, or are subject to abuse or abandonment by their parents. The most relevant forms of relief from removal are discussed below.

Asylum. Any alien—regardless of age[59]—may be eligible for asylum if the alien is unable or unwilling to return to his/her home country due to a well-founded fear of persecution on account of race, religion, nationality, political opinion, or membership in a particular social group.[60] An alien granted asylum may be eligible to work in the United States and adjust to LPR status.[61] In general, an alien can either apply for asylum "affirmatively" with U.S. Citizenship and Immigration Services (USCIS) within DHS or "defensively" in the context of removal proceedings before an immigration judge. However, Section 208 of the INA mandates that asylum officers within USCIS have initial jurisdiction over any asylum claim made by a UAC even if the UAC is in removal proceedings.[62] In addition, other provisions of federal law make it easier for UACs to be granted asylum on account of persecution.[63] For further discussion, see also "Can UACs obtain asylum due to gang violence in their home countries?".

SIJ Status. As previously noted (see "What is the difference between being a UAC and having Special Immigrant Juvenile (SIJ) status?"), some alien children without lawful status may be eligible for SIJ status, and, on the basis of this status, become LPRs.[64] Eligibility for SIJ status is limited to juveniles who, among other things, (1) have been declared by a state court to be a dependent on the court, or have been legally placed by the court with a state or an appointed private entity; (2) are unable to reunite with one or more parents on account of abuse, abandonment, or neglect; and (3) have been determined not to have his/her best interest served by being returned to his/her native country or country of last habitual residence.[65] The availability of an immigrant visa for aliens who obtain SIJ status is subject to the numerical cap on the allocation of immigrant visas for "special immigrants" (a category that includes several types of aliens in addition to those with SIJ status).[66]

Nonimmigrant Visa for Victims of Trafficking and Other Crimes. Alien children without immigration status could also be eligible for nonimmigrant visas allowing them to temporarily remain in the country (and potentially adjust to LPR status) if they are the victims of trafficking or certain other crimes. The INA provides that an alien may be granted a nonimmigrant visa (commonly referred to as a "T visa") if he or she is a victim of a severe form of trafficking, and satisfies at least one other specified requirement, such as being under the age of 18.[67] A T visa generally allows an alien to live in the United States for up to four years (subject to extension in limited cases), and the alien may apply for adjustment to LPR status after three years.[68] Up to 5,000 T visas may be issued per year.[69]

A separate nonimmigrant visa (commonly referred to as a "U visa") is available for aliens who (1) have suffered substantial physical or mental abuse on account of being victims of specified criminal activities;[70] (2) possess information regarding the criminal activity; and (3) have been or are likely to be helpful in a law enforcement investigation or prosecution of such activity.[71] A U visa may remain valid for up to four years (subject to extension in limited circumstances), and the visa-holder may apply for adjustment to LPR status after three years.[72] Up to 10,000 U visas may be issued per year.[73]

May Children without Immigration Status Be Released from DHS or HHS Custody?

DHS and HHS maintain custody over children without immigration status for different purposes. In the case of DHS, the primary purpose is to secure the child's presence at removal proceedings and during the execution of a final order of removal.[74] The purpose of HHS obtaining custody over UACs is generally not focused upon immigration enforcement, but instead to provide UACs with temporary shelter care and protect them from trafficking and other forms of exploitation.[75]

As a general matter, individual aliens placed in removal proceedings by DHS are potentially subject to detention, but may also be released on bond or parole—which here refers to release from custody, not entry into the United States—unless they fall under a category subject to mandatory detention.[76] DHS regulations and the *Flores* settlement agreement provide criteria for when juveniles in removal proceedings may be released from custody. The *Flores* settlement agreement establishes a "general policy" favoring the release of children from detention.[77] However, both the agreement and DHS regulations recognize that release is not required when DHS determines that the juvenile's continued detention is necessary to ensure his/her safety or the safety of others, or is required to secure the juvenile's presence at immigration removal proceedings.[78] DHS regulations provide that a juvenile may be released, in order of preference, to a parent, legal guardian, or other adult relative (brother, sister, aunt, uncle, or grandparent) who is not presently in DHS detention, another adult individual or entity who is designated by a parent or guardian in DHS custody and who agrees to care for the juvenile and ensure his/her presence at removal proceedings; or (in unusual and compelling circumstances) another adult individual or entity designated by DHS who agrees to care for the child and ensure his/her presence at removal proceedings.[79] Additionally, in cases where a juvenile is detained by DHS along with a parent, legal guardian, or adult family member, DHS may on a case-by-case basis opt to release the juvenile and accompanying adult from detention simultaneously.[80]

As noted earlier (see "Which federal agencies have primary responsibility for maintaining custody of alien children without immigration status?"), federal statute designates HHS's ORR with responsibility for the care and custody of UACs, other than certain arriving UACs from Canada and Mexico who have been immediately and voluntarily returned to their home countries.[81] When functions formerly handled by immigration authorities concerning UACs were transferred to HHS via the Homeland Security Act of 2002, HHS also became subject to the terms of the *Flores* settlement agreement.[82] Section 235 of the TVPRA provided further guidance concerning HHS standards for the care and control of UACs within the agency's custody.[83]

Following the transfer of a UAC to the custody of HHS's ORR, the UAC is generally released shortly thereafter to the physical custody of an ORR-contracted care facility.[84] The type of facility (e.g., shelter care, secure care, or foster care) may depend upon the particular needs of the UAC, the UAC's age, and whether the UAC poses a flight risk or a danger to himself/herself or others.[85] UACs remain in the legal custody of the federal government even though they may be temporary placed in the physical custody of a licensed care provider.[86] UACs could potentially remain in such facilities pending culmination of removal proceedings against them (at which point they may be removed from the United States); until they turn 18 (at which point they may be turned over to DHS custody, provided that DHS has initiated removal proceedings against them);[87] or until such times as ORR finds a parent, legal guardian, or other entity who may take custody of the UAC, in accordance with the terms of the *Flores* settlement agreement.[88]

The Secretary of HHS must consent to the jurisdiction of a juvenile court before the court may declare a child in HHS custody to be a dependent of the court or before the court may legally commit or place the juvenile in the custody of a state agency or a court-appointed person or entity.[89] As previously noted, such action by a state court is necessary before a juvenile can be granted SIJ status.[90]

What Is the "Best Interest of the Child" Standard, and How Does It Apply to Immigration Detention and Removal Decisions?

As the term suggests, the "best interest of the child" standard prioritizes an affected child's interests in the context of adjudication or other decision-making processes. The standard is typically employed by courts or administrative bodies considering issues implicating a child's welfare, including child custody and placement decisions.[91] There is no uniform consensus as to the particular factors that should be considered (or the weight given to each of these factors) when applying the "best interest of the child standard," and application of the standard can vary depending upon the context.[92]

The "best interest of the child" standard generally does not provide legal guidance as to whether or not a child is subject to removal.[93] A 2007 guidance document issued by the DOJ's Executive Office of Immigration Review (EOIR) concerning immigration court cases involving UACs notes the following:

> Issues of law—questions of admissibility, eligibility for relief, etc.—are governed by the Immigration and Nationality Act and the regulations. The concept of "best interest of the child" does not negate the statute or the regulatory delegation of the Attorney General's authority, and cannot provide a basis for providing relief not sanctioned by law.[94]

The "best interest of the child" standard may, however, inform the conduct of immigration removal proceedings,[95] even if the standard is not relevant to a determination of whether the child is removable. A child's interests are also relevant to other determinations by immigration authorities, including when or whether to release a child without immigration status from detention during the course of removal proceedings (though consideration of this interest is not dispositive, and it may be overcome by competing government interests, including ensuring the child's presence at removal hearings).[96] As noted above (see "What is the difference between being a UAC and having Special Immigrant Juvenile (SIJ) status?"), in determining an alien child's eligibility for SIJ status, immigration authorities must consider whether it would be in the child's best interest not to be repatriated to his/her home country.[97] However, other criteria must also be satisfied for a child to be deemed eligible for SIJ status.[98]

On the other hand, the "best interest of the child" standard is statutorily required to be considered by ORR in certain decisions involving UACs placed in its custody. In 2008, Congress mandated that UACs placed in ORR custody "be promptly placed in the least restrictive setting that is in the best interest of the child."[99]

Can UACs Obtain Asylum due to Gang Violence in Their Home Countries?

Some UACs could potentially be found to be eligible for asylum as a result of gang-related violence in their home countries, although the existence of such violence is not, in itself, a basis for asylum.[100] Rather, eligibility for asylum is determined on a case-by-case basis, with the individual alien applying for asylum having the burden of establishing that he/she is unable or unwilling to return to his/her home country because of persecution, or a well-founded fear of persecution, on account of race, religion, nationality, political opinion, or membership in a particular social group.[101] *Persecution* is not defined by either the INA or its implementing regulations, but has been construed to mean "the infliction of suffering or harm upon those who differ (in race, religion or political opinion) in a way regarded as offensive. ... [It is] an extreme concept that does not include every sort of treatment our society regards as offensive."[102]

Generalized violence or lawlessness may be distinguished from persecution,[103] as may be harms that are not seen as arising from the actions of the government or entities whom the government cannot or will not control.[104] Any persecution must also be "on account of" a protected ground (i.e., race, religion, etc.), a phrase which has been taken to mean that the protected ground serves as "at least one central reason for the persecution."[105]

Those seeking asylum based on gang-related violence have often asserted persecution on account of membership in a particular social group or, less commonly, political opinion (i.e., an actual or imputed political opinion that they are opposed to the gangs).[106] The relevant social group has been defined in various ways—including (1) those who oppose (or are taking "concrete" or "active" steps to oppose) the gangs' activities;[107] (2) those who resist attempts to recruit them to the gang;[108] (3) former gang members who have renounced their membership;[109] (3) witnesses who have testified against the gangs,[110] and (4) families that have been affected by gang violence[111]—and with various degrees of success. In a number of cases, administrative and judicial tribunals have declined to recognize the proposed social group because it is amorphous, and the individuals making up the group would not be perceived as a group by the society in question.[112] However, such determinations generally reflect the tribunals' view of the evidence that the alien offered regarding social perceptions in his/her home society,[113] not *per se* rules as to what constitutes a particular social group.[114] In other cases, individual aliens' claims regarding their treatment at the hands of their alleged persecutors are not seen as credible, for example, because of inconsistencies in their stories.[115] Some aliens may also be statutorily barred from receiving asylum under the INA, although such bars seem unlikely to affect UACs who are not former gang members.[116]

UACs are treated the same as other aliens in terms of applications for asylum, with two notable exceptions, previously noted (see "Are children without immigration status eligible for relief from removal?"). First, all applications for asylum involving UACs must be heard by USCIS, regardless of whether the application involves an alien currently in removal proceedings. Claims involving aliens in proceedings—widely known as "defensive applications"—are otherwise heard exclusively by immigration judges, with only claims by aliens not in removal proceedings (i.e., "affirmative applications") being heard by USCIS.[117] However, Section 208 of the INA and its implementing regulations require that both defensive and affirmative applications by UACs be heard by USCIS.[118] Second, an alien's minority status could constitute an "extraordinary circumstance" that would permit an application for asylum to be filed more than one year after the alien's arrival in the United States.[119] Claims filed more than one year after arrival are otherwise barred absent the existence of "changed circumstances that materially affect the applicant's eligibility for asylum."[120]

Rights, Privileges, and Benefits

Do UACs Have a Right to Counsel at the Government's Expense in Removal Proceedings?

Two separate provisions of federal law address UACs' access to legal counsel. One provision— Section 235 of the TVPRA, as amended—generally requires the Secretary of HHS to "ensure" that UACs in HHS or DHS custody "have counsel to represent them in legal proceedings or matters and protect them from mistreatment, exploitation, and trafficking."[121] The other provision—Section 462 of the Homeland Security Act, as amended—requires the Director of the ORR at HHS to develop a plan to "ensure that qualified and independent legal counsel is timely appointed to represent the interests of each child."[122] However, because both provisions describe such access as being "consistent with" Section 292 of the INA and other provisions of federal law, they have not been construed as requiring the appointment of counsel at the government's expense since these provisions require that any such counsel be "at no expense to the Government."[123]

In several cases, UACs and their advocates have challenged Section 292 and the government's corresponding failure to provide counsel to UACs in removal proceedings, including on the grounds that it violates the Due Process Clause of the U.S. Constitution.[124] These challenges sometimes note that children in other types of civil proceedings have been found to have a categorical right to counsel at the government's expense, regardless of their individual circumstances. They often also note that the consequences of potential removal for aliens are comparable to the consequences of these other proceedings.[125] Courts have, to date, rejected these arguments, declining to recognize a categorical right to counsel at the government's expense for UACs or other aliens. However, at least four federal courts of appeal[126] have opined that the Due Process Clause could potentially require the appointment of counsel on a case-by-case basis for individual aliens who are incapable of representing themselves due to "age, ignorance, or mental capacity."[127] Section 504 of the Rehabilitation Act has also been construed in such a way that it could result in the appointment of counsel at the government's expense for unrepresented immigration detainees with "serious mental disorders or conditions that may render them mentally incompetent to represent themselves in immigration proceedings."[128] Certain UACs could potentially be encompassed by the protections of Section 504.

Does Section 292 of The INA Bar the Federal Government from Paying for Counsel for UAC?

The federal government's recent announcement that it will award $2 million in grants to enroll "about 100 lawyers and paralegals" to represent children in immigration proceedings[129] has prompted questions about whether doing so is barred by Section 292 of the INA. As previously noted (see "Do UACs have a right to counsel at the government's expense in removal proceedings?"), Section 292 generally governs aliens' right to counsel, and provides that,

> In any removal proceedings before an immigration judge and in any appeal proceedings before the Attorney General from any such removal proceedings, the person concerned shall have the privilege of being represented (at no expense to the Government) by such counsel ... as he shall choose.[130]

Some have previously suggested that this provision, by itself or in conjunction with 5 U.S.C. §3106—which generally bars agencies from "employ[ing] an attorney or counsel for the conduct of litigation in which the United States ... is a party"—precludes the government from providing or otherwise paying for aliens' counsel in removal proceedings.[131] Those making this argument seemingly construe the language about aliens' "privilege" to have counsel at their own expense to mean that the government may not pay for counsel for them. However, this interpretation does not appear to have been adopted by any court, and other interpretations could be advanced. In particular, an argument could be made that these provisions only restrict aliens' ability to claim an entitlement to counsel at the government's expense, and do not preclude the government from paying for aliens' counsel pursuant to other provisions of law or at its discretion.[132]

Are There Legal Requirements Concerning Consular Notification and Access When an Alien Child Is Taken into Federal Custody?

Along with the vast majority of countries, the United States is a party to the Vienna Convention on Consular Relations (VCCR), a multilateral agreement codifying consular practices originally governed by customary practice and bilateral agreements.[133] Pursuant to Article 36 of the VCCR, when a national of a State party (i.e., country) is arrested or otherwise detained in another State party, appropriate authorities within the arresting State must inform the person arrested "without delay" of the ability to have his/her consulate notified. The VCCR does not require the arresting State to notify the appropriate consular officials in every instance; rather, it requires the arresting State to notify the foreign national in its custody that he/she has the option of having his/her consulate notified. A foreign consular officer also is provided the right to communicate and be provided access to a detained national, including the ability to visit the national in the detention facility and arrange legal representation.[134] DHS regulations require that "[e]very detained alien shall be notified that he or she may communicate with the consular or diplomatic officers of the country of his or her nationality in the United States."[135]

The United States also has bilateral agreements with a number of countries that require consular notification in the event that one of the parties arrests a national of the other party.[136] Most UACs encountered by CBP along the U.S.-Mexico border are from countries (including Mexico) that are parties to the VCCR but do not have separate agreements requiring mandatory consular notification.[137] The VCCR identifies consular functions as including "safeguarding ... the interests of minors and other persons lacking full capacity who are nationals of the sending State, particularly where any guardianship or trusteeship is required with respect to such persons."[138] Some have argued that, consistent with the VCCR's recognition of this function, consular officers should be notified whenever a UAC or other alien child is taken into custody by immigration authorities,[139] but current DHS regulations provide for mandatory consular notification only when a bilateral agreement expressly requires it.[140]

The United States may also enter into both legally binding and nonlegal arrangements with foreign countries concerning the repatriation of their nationals. In recent years, DHS and local ICE or CBP field offices have entered (nonlegal)[141] arrangements concerning the repatriation of Mexican nationals, including UACs. These arrangements typically call for notification of Mexican consular officials and other Mexican authorities when a UAC is to be repatriated, and provide for repatriation to occur during daylight hours.[142]

In addition to consular notification requirements relating to the detention of a foreign national, the VCCR also provides that appropriate authorities within the host country notify the appropriate consular post "without delay of any case where the appointment of a guardian or trustee appears to be in the interests of a minor or other person lacking full capacity who is a national of the sending State."[143]

Are UACs Eligible for Deferred Action for Childhood Arrivals?

UACs who entered the United States in FY2014 are generally not eligible for deferred action—a type of temporary relief from removal, the receipt of which can result in aliens receiving work authorization and certain public benefits—under the Deferred Action for Childhood Arrivals (DACA) initiative.[144] Pursuant to the DHS guidelines regarding DACA, eligibility is limited to aliens who have resided in the United States since June 15, 2007, and who were physically present in the United States on June 15, 2012.[145] Such residence must have been "continuous," which is generally construed to mean that any absences from the United States are "brief, causal, and innocent."[146] Thus, even if individual UACs happened to be re-entering the United States after a prior period of presence, the requirement as to continuous residence could present issues.

Immigration officials may, however, still grant deferred action to aliens outside of DACA if they have prioritized other aliens for removal, or if humanitarian factors weigh in favor of allowing individual aliens to remain in the United States.[147]

End Notes

[1] See, e.g., Julia Preston, Migrants Flow in South Texas, as Do Rumors, N.Y. TIMES, June 16, 2014, available at http://www.nytimes.com/2014/06/17/us/migrants-flow-in-south-texas-as-do-rumors.html?emc=edit_th_20140617&nl=todaysheadlines&nlid=5753597&_r=1 (reporting that 47,000 UACs have been apprehended along the southern border since October 2013, and the number may double by the end of FY2014); Mario Trujillo, White House Scrambles to Keep Up with Child Immigrant Surge, THE HILL, June 20, 2014, available at http://thehill.com/homenews/ administration/210093-white-house-scrambles-to-keep-up-with-child-immigrant-surge.

[2] P.L. 107-296, §462, 116 Stat. 2202-2205 (Nov. 25, 2002) (codified, as amended, at 6 U.S.C. §279).

[3] See generally Cortez-Vasquez v. Holder, 440 Fed. App'x 295, 298 (5th Cir. 2011) (alien minor "accompanied by his adult sister" not a UAC); Bunikyte v. Chertoff, No. A-07-CA-164-SS, No. A-07-CA-165-SS, No. A-07-CA-166-SS, 2007 U.S. Dist. LEXIS 26166, at *14-*15 (W.D. Tex., Apr. 9, 2007) (parents generally deemed responsible for the care of minor children when parents are detained with minor children).

[4] See Immigration Act of 1990, P.L. 101-649, §153, 104 Stat. 5005-5006 (Nov. 29, 1990) (codified, as amended, at INA §101(a)(27)(J), 8 U.S.C. §1101(a)(27)(J)); 8 C.F.R. §204.11(c). Currently, the age limit pertains to the date on which the application for SIJ status is filed, not that when it is granted. See generally 8 U.S.C. §1232(d)(6). Under an earlier version of this rule, some aliens "aged out" while their petitions for SIJ status were pending.

[5] INA §101(a)(27)(J)(i), 8 U.S.C. §1101(a)(27)(J)(i); 8 C.F.R. §204.11(a) (definition of eligible for long-term foster care) & (c)(3)-(4) (eligibility criteria). The INA is codified in Title 8 of the United States Code, and references to it in this report also include references to the corresponding sections of Title 8. However, Title 8 also includes provisions that are not part of the INA. Citations to such provisions will have no corresponding citation to the INA.

[6] INA §101(a)(27)(J)(ii), 8 U.S.C. §1101(a)(27)(A)(ii); 8 C.F.R. §204.11(c)(6).

[7] 8 C.F.R. §204.11(c)(5) (requiring that the declaration of dependency on the court and eligibility for long-term foster care not have been vacated, terminated, or otherwise ended). A further constraint upon the granting of SIJ status is that the Department of Health and Human Services (HHS) must specifically consent to a juvenile court's jurisdiction to determine the "custody status or placement" of an alien in HHS custody. See INA §101(a)(27)(J)(iii)(I), 8 U.S.C. §1101(a)(27)(A)(iii)(I). In the past, questions were raised about federal agencies' practices in handling juveniles' requests for consent to juvenile court jurisdiction. See, e.g., Perez-Olano v. Gonzalez, 2008 U.S. Dist. LEXIS 85675, at *46-*52 (C.D. Cal., Jan. 8, 2008) (invalidating, on statutory interpretation grounds, U.S. Immigration and Customs Enforcement's (ICE's) practice of requiring its specific consent to all SIJ-predicate orders); Perez-Olano v. Holder, Case No. CV 05-3604, Settlement Agreement (C.D. Cal., May 4, 2010) (copy on file with the authors) (generally requiring federal officials to expedite requests for consent to juvenile court jurisdiction). Such concerns may have been allayed as a result of the litigation and settlement agreement noted here.

[8] See 8 C.F.R. §204.11(d). Aliens whose petitions are denied have the right to appeal. Id. at §204.11(e).

[9] INA §245(g) & (h)(1), 8 U.S.C. §1255(g) & (h)(1) (SIJs deemed to have been paroled); INA §245(h)(2), 8 U.S.C. §1255(h)(2) (applications for LPR status). Certain grounds of inadmissibility are or may be waived for aliens granted SIJ status. See infra note 98. Natural

or prior adoptive parents of aliens provided SIJ status may not be accorded any right, privilege or status, by virtue of such parentage, under the INA, although other close natural or prior adoptive relatives (e.g., siblings) are not similarly barred from seeking certain rights, privileges or status by virtue of their relationship to an alien with SIJ status. INA §101(a)(27)(J)(iii)(II), 8 U.S.C. §1101(a)(27)(J)(iii)(II).

[10] See generally Flores v. Reno, Case No. CV 85-4544-RJK(Px), Stipulated Settlement Agreement (C.D. Cal., 1997) (copy on file with the authors). In a number of places, the settlement agreement refers to "unaccompanied minors." However, the plaintiff class is defined as "[a]ll minors who are detained in the legal custody of the INS," and at least one court has expressly construed the agreement to apply to minors who are detained with their parents. See Bunikyte, 2007 U.S. Dist. LEXIS 26166, at *8. The agreement also refers to the Immigration and Naturalization Service (INS), but has been found to be binding upon its successor agencies (such as DHS). Bunikyte, 2007 U.S. Dist. LEXIS 26166, at *50. See also infra at note 33.

[11] See Reno v. Flores, 507 U.S. 292, 295-296 (1993).

[12] Id. at 301-303.

[13] See Stipulated Settlement Agreement, supra note 10, at 3.

[14] Id. at 11.

[15] Id. at 12.A.

[16] Id. at 14-15.

[17] Id. at 11. Similarly, the agreement grants federal officials greater latitude in the event of an "emergency" or "influx of minors into the United States." Id. at 12.A. However, in light of subsequently enacted legislation (see "Which federal agencies have primary responsibility for maintaining custody of alien children without immigration status?"), this exception seems most likely to be relevant to accompanied minors. The agreement defines an emergency as "any act or event that prevents the placement of minors pursuant to Paragraph 19 [i.e., with licensed facilities]" within the three- to five-day time frame contemplated by the agreement, and an influx as occurring whenever federal officials have in their custody more than 130 minors eligible for placement in a licensed program. See id. at 12.B.

[18] See, e.g., Fabian v. Dunn, No. SA-08-cv-269-XR, 2009 U.S. Dist. LEXIS 26552 (W.D. Tex., Aug. 14, 2009); Walding v. United States, No. SA-08-CA-124-XR, 2009 U.S. Dist. LEXIS 26546 (W.D. Tex. Mar. 31, 2009).

[19] Walding, 2009 U.S. Dist. LEXIS 26546, at *74-*75.

[20] Id. at *56.

[21] For example, the Flores agreement makes provisions for the government to have additional time to transfer alien minors from the facility of their immediate post-arrest placement to a licensed facility in the event of an "emergency" or "influx of minors". See Stipulated Settlement Agreement, supra note 10, at 12a. However, the William Wilberforce Trafficking Victims Protection Reauthorization Act (TVPRA) of 2008 (P.L. 110-457), as amended, does not include similar provisions.

[22] See Stipulated Settlement Agreement, supra note 10, at 40.

[23] See Flores v. Reno, Case No. CV 85-4544-RJK(Px), Stipulation Extending the Settlement Agreement and for Other Purposes, and Order Thereon (C.D. Cal., Dec. 7, 2001) (copy on file with the authors).

[24] See 8 U.S.C. §1182(a)(7)(A)(i). Individual UACs could potentially also be inadmissible on other grounds. See generally INA §212, 8 U.S.C. §1182 (establishing health-, crime-, and security-related grounds of inadmissibility). See also INA §101(a)(13)(A), 8 U.S.C. §1101(a)(13)(A) (defining admission). Aliens encountered between ports of entry raise

somewhat different issues. Some UACs may also be unlawfully present within the interior of the United States when encountered by immigration officers.

[25] INA §212(a)(7)(A)(i), 8 U.S.C. §1182(a)(7)(A)(i). Under the INA, aliens are presumed to be immigrants unless they fall into designated categories (e.g., ambassadors, temporary visitors for business or pleasure). INA §101(a)(15), 8 U.S.C. §1101(a)(15). There are two exceptions to this general rule. One exception—permitting the waiver of the Section 212(a)(7) grounds of inadmissibility for aliens who are in possession of immigrant visas that, unbeknownst to them, are invalid—is generally inapplicable where UACs are concerned. INA §212(k), 8 U.S.C. §1182(k). The other exception permits the admission of aliens "as specifically provided in this Act." INA §212(a), 8 U.S.C. §1182.

[26] INA §101(a)(13)(A), 8 U.S.C. §1101(a)(13)(A).

[27] Prior to the enactment of the Illegal Immigration Reform and Immigrant Responsibility Act (IIRIRA) of 1996, Section 101(a)(13) of the INA defined entry in this way. Even after this definition of entry was stricken in 1996, similar constructions of the term have still been applied in other contexts. See, e.g., Matter of Rosas-Ramirez, 22 I. & N. Dec. 616 (1999) (discussing whether adjustment of status while within the United States constitutes an "admission" for purposes of Section 237(a)(2)(A)(iii) of the INA, and noting that admission is defined, in part, in terms of "entry").

[28] P.L. 110-457, §235, 122 Stat. 5074 (Dec. 23, 2008) (codified, as amended, at 8 U.S.C. §1232).

[29] 8 U.S.C. §1232(a)(2)(A).

[30] 8 U.S.C. §1232(a)(3) & (b)(3). These provisions have also been taken to mean that UACs must generally be retained in federal custody for at least for a brief time, instead of being released immediately to families or community groups.

[31] See 8 U.S.C. §1182(d)(5)(A). See also INA §101(a)(13)(B), 8 U.S.C. §1101(a)(13)(B) (aliens paroled under Section 212(d)(5) "shall not be considered to have been admitted").

[32] Section 208 of the INA specifically permits arriving aliens to apply for asylum, "irrespective of [their] status." INA §208(a)(1), 8 U.S.C. §1158(a)(1).

[33] For many decades, the INS within the Department of Justice (DOJ) was delegated responsibility for immigration enforcement activities. Following the establishment of DHS pursuant to the Homeland Security Act of 2002 (P.L. 107- 296), the INS was abolished and its enforcement functions were transferred to DHS. See 6 U.S.C. §§251, 291.

[34] Interior immigration enforcement activities, including apprehending and effectuating the removal of aliens within the United States who are believed to be present in violation of federal immigration laws, are primarily the responsibility of ICE within DHS.

[35] In particular, CBP's Office of Field Operations is primarily responsible for border security matters at ports of entry, while U.S. land borders between ports of entry are monitored by agents from CBP's Office of Border Patrol.

[36] 6 U.S.C. §279.

[37] 6 U.S.C §279(b)(1)(A). See also 8 U.S.C. §1232(b), (d).

[38] See, e.g., Dep't of Health & Human Servs., Office of Refugee Resettlement, About Unaccompanied Children's Services, available at http://www.acf.hhs.gov/programs/orr/programs/ucs/about (last accessed: June 26, 2014). See also Bunikyte, 2007 U.S. Dist. LEXIS 26166, at *25-*27 (finding that a state's granting a licensing exception to a facility does not discharge the government's obligation under the Flores settlement agreement to house detained minors in licensed facilities, and noting the steps that the Berks Family Residential Center took to obtain licensing, given that it did not fit within the existing taxonomy of state licensees).

[39] See 8 U.S.C. §1232(a)(5)(D) (placement of UACs in removal proceedings).

[40] See 8 C.F.R. §241.3(a) (aliens ordered removed shall be taken into DHS custody pursuant to a warrant of removal).

[41] An arriving alien may, in limited circumstances, also be released from DHS custody and paroled into the United States under INA §212(d)(5), if parole is justified by "urgent humanitarian reasons" or "significant public benefit." See 8 C.F.R. §212.5(b) (concerning parole of arriving juvenile aliens).

[42] 8 U.S.C. §1232(a)(2).

[43] See 8 C.F.R. §235.4 (DHS custody over aliens who withdraw their application for admission).

[44] 8 U.S.C. §1232(a)(4). As previously noted, the Flores agreement would generally govern on specific questions not otherwise addressed in statute, and as to populations not covered by the statute (i.e., accompanied alien children).

[45] 8 U.S.C. §1232(b)(3). The Flores agreement also generally requires that UACs be transferred from "placement" with DHS following initial arrest to temporary placement in a licensed program (pending release or the conclusion of immigration proceedings) within 72 hours. See Stipulated Settlement Agreement, supra note 10, at 12a, 19.

[46] Indeed, plaintiffs in at least one case have alleged that the INA requires that any alien unlawfully present in the United States be placed in removal proceedings. A federal district court initially found for the plaintiffs in this case. See Crane v. Napolitano, 920 F. Supp. 2d 724, 740-741 (N.D. Tex. 2013). However, the court subsequently found that it lacked jurisdiction. Crane, No. 3:12-cv-03247-O, Order (N.D. Tex., July 31, 2013) (copy on file with the authors).

[47] INA §235(b), 8 U.S.C. §1225(b).

[48] 8 U.S.C. §1232(a)(5)(D) (requiring placement of UACs in formal removal proceedings, except when they are arriving from Canada or Mexico and have agreed to be voluntarily returned).

[49] Id.; INA §240, 8 U.S.C. §1229a. These proceedings are adversarial in nature and are conducted before an immigration judge within the DOJ's Executive Office of Immigration Review (EOIR). An alien placed in such proceedings may, among other things, examine evidence and contest the government's case against his/her removability, present evidence on his/her own behalf, cross-examine witnesses, and be represented by counsel (generally) at no expense to the government. Id. Decisions by an immigration judge may be appealed to EOIR's Board of Immigration Appeals (BIA)—the highest administrative tribunal responsible for interpreting and applying immigration law—and, in many cases, to a federal court.

[50] 8 U.S.C. §1232(a)(5)(D) & (c)(5). The INA provides, however, that aliens placed in removal proceedings have a privilege of being represented by counsel at no expense to the government. INA §292, 8 U.S.C. §1362. See "Do UACs have a right to counsel at the government's expense in removal proceedings?".

[51] 8 U.S.C. §1232(a)(4). An alien granted voluntary departure must typically pay the costs associated with departing the United States. INA §240B(a)(1), 8 U.S.C. §1229C(a)(1).

[52] INA §235(a)(1), 8 U.S.C. §1225(a)(1). DHS regulations generally define an arriving alien as "an applicant for admission coming or attempting to come into the United States at a port-of-entry, or an alien seeking transit through the United States at a port-of-entry, or an alien interdicted in international or United States waters and brought into the United States.... " 8 C.F.R. §1.2.

[53] 8 U.S.C. §1232(a)(2).

[54] Among other things, an arriving alien who is permitted to withdraw his/her application for admission must generally depart immediately from the United States, while an alien granted voluntary departure is often permitted to remain in the country for a specified period.

Compare INA §235(a)(4), 8 U.S.C. §1225(a)(4) (providing that an alien permitted to withdraw his/her application will "depart immediately") with INA §240B(a)(2) & (b)(2), 8 U.S.C. §1229C(a)(2) & (b)(2) (specifying time period when alien may be permitted to voluntarily depart). A violation of a voluntary departure order may result in civil monetary penalties and other consequences not applicable to persons who immediately depart following the withdrawal of an application of admission. See INA §240B(d), 8 U.S.C. §1229C(d).

[55] Severe form of trafficking is defined to cover both sex and labor trafficking. See 22 U.S.C. §7102(9).

[56] 8 U.S.C. §1232(a)(2).

[57] Id.

[58] UACs also enjoy another type of protection as to removal, in that immigration judges may not accept admissions of removability from unrepresented UACs. See 8 C.F.R. §1240.10(c) ("The immigration judge shall not accept an admission of removability from an unrepresented respondent who is incompetent or under the age of 18 and is not accompanied by an attorney or legal representative, a near relative, legal guardian, or friend."). This bar does not, however, extend to admissions to factual allegations, because minors under the age of 16 are "not presumed incapable of understanding the context of the allegations and determining whether they are true." Matter of Amaya-Castro, 21 I. & N. Dec. 583 (BIA 1996). See also Gonzales-Reyes v. Holder, 313 Fed. App'x 690, 696-697 (5th Cir. 2009).

[59] See, e.g., Gonzalez v. Reno, 212 F.3d 1338, 1348, 1351 (11th Cir. 2000) (no per se bar to a six-year-old filing an application for asylum, since Section 208(a) of the INA states that "[a]ny alien ... may apply", although an application on behalf of such a young child that is opposed by his/her parent may be viewed as a nullity).

[60] INA §208(b)(1)(A), 8 U.S.C. §1158(b)(1)(A)(permitting the granting of asylum to eligible aliens who fall within the definition of refugee found at INA §101(a)(42), 8 U.S.C. §1101(a)(42)).

[61] INA §§208(c), 209(b); 8 U.S.C. §§1158(c), 1159(b).

[62] INA §208(b)(3)(C), 8 U.S.C. §1158(b)(3)(C). If the UAC's asylum application is denied, he/she may be placed in removal proceedings (in which the child may challenge the basis for the denial of the application).

[63] Specifically, unlike other asylum applicants, UACs may be eligible for asylum even if they could be removed, pursuant to a bilateral or multilateral agreement, to a third country where they would not face persecution and would have access to procedures by which to obtain asylum or equivalent temporary protection in that country. Additionally, UACs' asylum applications are not subject to the time bar that normally requires aliens to apply for asylum within one year of arriving in the United States. INA §208(a)(2)(E), 8 U.S.C. §1158(a)(2)(E), as added by Section 235(d)(7)(A) of the TVPRA (P.L. 110-457).

[64] See INA §§101(a)(27)(J), 203(b)(4), & 245(h); 8 U.S.C. §§101(a)(27)(J), 1153(b)(4), & 1255(h).

[65] INA §101(a)(27)(J), 8 U.S.C.§1101(a)(27)(J). There are other preconditions for SIJ status. See generally "What is the difference between being a UAC and having Special Immigrant Juvenile (SIJ) status?".

[66] See INA §203(b)(4), 8 U.S.C. §1253(b)(4) (providing for the allocation of immigration visas to "special immigrants," other than certain subcategories subject to separate requirements, is "a number not to exceed 7.1 percent of such worldwide level" of immigration visas for "employment-based immigrants" under INA §203(b)).

[67] INA §101(a)(15)(T), 8 U.S.C. §1101(a)(15)(T) (other potential qualifying factors include cooperating with a relevant law enforcement investigation or prosecution of acts of trafficking, or being unable to cooperate with such efforts on account of physical or psychological trauma). But see United States v. Resuleo-Flores, No. CR 11-0686 51, 2012 U.S. Dist. LEXIS 30201, at *27 (N.D. Cal., Mar. 7, 2012) (alien under the age of 16 who recanted her charges to the police could nonetheless be found to have cooperated with law enforcement given her initial reporting of the crime, especially as her guardians discouraged her from further cooperation).

[68] INA §214(o), 8 U.S.C. §1184(o); INA §245(l), 8 U.S.C. §1255(l).

[69] INA §214(o), 8 U.S.C. §1184(o).

[70] Covered criminal activities include, inter alia, domestic violence, rape, trafficking, kidnapping, involuntary servitude, and felonious assault. INA §101(a)(15)(U)(iii), 8 U.S.C. §1101(a)(15)(U)(iii).

[71] INA §101(a)(15)(U), 8 U.S.C. §1101(a)(15)(U). When the alien is a child under the age of 16, the eligibility requirements concerning law enforcement assistance may be performed by a parent, guardian, or next friend. Id.

[72] INA §214(p), 8 U.S.C. §1184(p).

[73] INA §245(m), 8 U.S.C. §1255(m).

[74] If DHS opts not to pursue immigration enforcement proceedings against an alien, the alien must be released from its custody.

[75] See 6 U.S.C. §279(b) (describing general functions with respect to UACs); 8 U.S.C. §1232(c) (requiring the establishment of policies and programs to protect UACs from trafficking and other harmful activities).

[76] INA §236(a), 8 U.S.C. §1226(a). The granting of parole (in the sense of release from custody) to aliens detained by immigration authorities pending a decision on their removal is understood to be distinct from the parole of arriving aliens into the United States under INA §212(d)(5) on account of urgent humanitarian reasons or a significant public benefit. See Matter of Castillo-Padilla, 25 I. & N. Dec. 257 (BIA 2010). See also 8 C.F.R. §212.5 (standards for parole of aliens into United States pursuant to INA §212(d)(5)).

[77] Stipulated Settlement Agreement, supra note 10, at 11.

[78] Id.; 8 C.F.R. §236.3(b).

[79] 8 C.F.R. §236.3(b).

[80] Id. But see Bunikyte, 2007 U.S. Dist. LEXIS 26166, at *49-*53 (rejecting the argument that the Flores agreement required that detained parents be released so that their children could be released with them).

[81] 6 U.S.C. §279; 8 U.S.C. §1232.

[82] 6 U.S.C. §552(a) (concerning continued recognition of "completed administrative actions", including agreements, made by agencies whose functions were transferred to other departments pursuant to the Homeland Security Act).

[83] 8 U.S.C. §1232.

[84] Stipulated Settlement Agreement, supra note 10, at 14. Paragraph 28.A of the Flores agreement requires the government to monitor contractors' performance to ensure that the terms of the agreement are met. See, e.g., Walding v. United States, 955 F. Supp. 2d 759, 781 (W.D. Tex. 2013). For a more detailed description of ORR's responsibility for UACs, see CRS Report R43599, Unaccompanied Alien Children: An Overview, by Lisa Seghetti, Alison Siskin, and Ruth Ellen Wasem; Olga Byrne & Elise Miller, Vera Institute of Justice, The Flow of Unaccompanied Children Through the Immigration System, at 8-21 (March 2012),

available at http://www.vera.org/sites/default/files/resources/ downloads/the-flow-of-unaccompanied-children-through-the-immigration-system.pdf.

[85] See CRS Report R43599, Unaccompanied Alien Children: An Overview, by Lisa Seghetti, Alison Siskin, and Ruth Ellen Wasem; Byrne and Miller, supra note 84, at 19. See also 8 U.S.C. §1232(c)(2) (generally requiring HHS to place UACs within its custody in "the least restrictive setting that is in the best interest of the child").

[86] See Dep't of Health & Human Services, Office of Refugee Resettlement, Notice of Grant Opportunity for Residential Services for Unaccompanied Children, at 2 (2014), available at http://www.acf.hhs.gov/grants/open/foa/files/HHS2014-ACF-ORR-ZU-0608_0.pdf ("UAC are in the legal custody of the Federal Government throughout their stay in ORR care but will be in the physical custody of the residential care provider.").

[87] 8 U.S.C. §1232(c)(2)(B). DHS is required to consider placing such persons "in the least restrictive setting available after taking into account the alien's danger to self, danger to the community, and risk of flight," and transferred persons are made eligible to participate in alternative to detention programs. Id.

[88] See Stipulated Settlement Agreement, supra note 10, at 12.A & 14.

[89] INA §101(a)(27)(J)(iii)(I), 8 U.S.C.§1101(a)(27)(J)(iii)(I).

[90] See supra at "What is the difference between being a UAC and having Special Immigrant Juvenile (SIJ) status?".

[91] See generally Dept. of Health & Human Services, Children's Bureau, Determining the Best Interests of the Child (last updated Nov. 2012) [hereinafter "HHS Overview of State Statutes"], available at https://www.childwelfare.gov/ systemwide/laws_policies/statutes/best_interest.pdf (providing overview of standard, its application, and various state statutes implementing the standard); Lynne Marie Kohm, Tracing the Foundations of the Best Interests of the Child Standard in American Jurisprudence, 10 J.L. & FAM. STUD. 376 (2008) (discussing origins and development of standard).

[92] See generally HHS Overview of State Statues, supra note 91 (identifying and discussing state laws providing guidance for application of "best interest of the child" standard); Kohm, supra note 91 (discussing judicial discretion in assessing and interpreting what serves a child's best interest).

[93] In 2002, a federal district court held that INA provisions concerning alien removal and relief from removal should be construed in a manner consistent with international agreements and customary international law, including "principles of customary international law that the best interests of the child must be considered where possible." Beharry v. Reno, 183 F. Supp. 2d 584 (E.D. N.Y. 2002). This ruling was subsequently vacated on jurisdictional grounds, 329 F.3d 51 (2d Cir. 2003). The BIA has held that customary international law does not afford an alien a remedy from removal above and beyond those forms of relief established by the INA, and that, even assuming arguendo that customary law could provide a basis for such relief, immigration judges have not been delegated authority to make such determinations by the Attorney General. See Matter of A–E–M–, 21 I. & N. Dec. 1157 (BIA 1998).

[94] Dep't of Justice, Exec. Office of Immigration Review, Office of the Chief Immigration Judge, Operating Policies and Procedures Memorandum 7-01, Guidelines for Immigration Court Cases Involving Unaccompanied Alien Children, at 4 (2007), available at http://www.justice. gov/eoir/efoia/ocij/oppm07/07-01.pdf.

[95] Id. ("[T]his concept is a factor that relates to the immigration judge's discretion in taking steps to ensure that a 'child-appropriate' hearing environment is established, allowing a child to discuss freely the elements and details of his or her claim.").

[96] See 8 C.F.R. §236.3 (DHS standards for releasing juveniles in removal proceedings from custody); Stipulated Settlement Agreement, supra note 10, at 14, 19, & Exhibit 1 (specifying conditions at the locations where children are held by immigration authorities, identifying a "general policy" favoring the release of children from custody, but providing that children are not required to be released when authorities believe that detention is necessary to secure the child's presence at removal proceedings or ensure the child's release does not pose a danger to the child or others).

[97] INA §101(a)(27)(J), 8 U.S.C. §1101(a)(27)(J).

[98] Id. (also requiring that an SIJ applicant (1) has been declared by a state court to be a dependent of the court, or to have been legally placed by the court with a state or an appointed private entity; and (2) is unable to reunite with one or more parents on account of abuse, abandonment, or neglect). Moreover, some grounds of inadmissibility may bar an alien with SIJ status from adjusting to LPR status. See INA §245(h), 8 U.S.C. §1255(h) (exempting SIJs from being ineligible for adjustment of status on certain inadmissibility grounds, and permitting immigration authorities to waive other inadmissibility grounds).

[99] 8 U.S.C. §1232(c)(2)(A). The requirement that children be placed in the "least restrictive setting" mirrors language found in the Flores settlement agreement. See, e.g., Settlement Agreement, supra note 10, at 23.

[100] Compare INA §101(a)(42), 8 U.S.C. §1101(a)(42) ("For purpose of determinations under this Act, a person who has been forced to abort a pregnancy or to undergo involuntary sterilization, or who has been persecuted for failure or refusal to undergo such a procedure or for other resistance to a coercive population control program, shall be deemed to have been persecuted on account of political opinion.").

[101] See generally INA §208(b)(1)(B)(i), 8 U.S.C. §1158(b)(1)(B)(i). Certain aliens arriving at the U.S. border or a port of entry are required to show a "credible fear" of persecution in order to avoid removal or return to their home country. See INA §235(a)(2) & (b)(1)(B)(ii), 8 U.S.C. §1225(a)(2) & (b)(1)(B)(ii) (stowaways and certain arriving aliens, respectively); 8 U.S.C. §1232(a)(2)(A) (UACs from contiguous countries). However, with the exception of UACs from contiguous countries, credible fear generally does not factor into the asylum process since UACs are subject to formal removal proceedings under Section 240 of the INA, not expedited removal under Section 235. See 8 U.S.C. §1232(a)(5)(D)(i).

[102] Ghaly v. INS, 58 F.3d 1425, 1431 (9th Cir. 1995). See also Osaghae v. INS, 942 F.2d 1160, 1163 (7th Cir. 1991) ("'Persecution' means, in immigration law, punishment for political, religious, or other reasons that our country does not recognize as legitimate."); H.R. REP. NO. 95-1452, at 5, as reprinted in 1978 U.S.C.C.A.N. 4700, 4704 ("Generally [the] case law has described persecution as the infliction of suffering or harm under government sanction, upon persons who differ in a way regarded as offense (e.g., race, religion, political opinion, etc.), in a manner condemned by civilized governments.").

[103] See, e.g., Jutus v. Holder, 723 F.3d 105 (1st Cir. 2013) (application denied where alien noted only "widespread societal violence and inadequate police and judicial protection" in Guatemala); Escobar v. Holder, 698 F.3d 36, 39 (1st Cir. 2012) ("[B]eing a target for thieves on account of perceived wealth ... is merely a condition of living where crime is rampant and poorly controlled.").

[104] Compare Fuentes-Chavarria, No. 13-9503, 2014 U.S. App. LEXIS 6956, at *11 (10th Cir., Apr. 15, 2014) (evidence did not establish that the feared harms would occur "on behalf of the government or with the government's willful blindness") with Karki v. Holder, 715 F.3d 792, 807 (10th Cir. 2013) (in light of circumstances, government's failure to prevent or

prosecute acts of a political party was sufficient to show the government would likely acquiesce).

[105] Crespin-Valladares v. Holder, 632 F.3d 117, 127 (4th Cir. 2011). A "central reason," in turn, has been described as one that is more than "incidental, tangential, superficial, or subordinate to another reason for harm." Quineros-Mendoza v. Holder, 556 F.3d 159, 164 (4th Cir. 2009) (quoting Matter of J-B-N-, 24 I. & N. Dec. 208, 214 (BIA 2007)).

[106] See, e.g., Castillo Sanchez v. U.S. Attorney General, 523 Fed. App'x 682 (11th Cir. 2013).

[107] See, e.g., Pirir-Boc v. Holder, No. 09-73671, 2014 U.S. App. LEXIS 8577 (9th Cir., May 7, 2014).

[108] See, e.g., Flores Munoz v. Holder, No. 13-60601, 2014 U.S. App. LEXIS 8974 (5th Cir., May 14, 2014); Matter of S-E-G-, 24 I. & N. Dec. 579 (2008).

[109] See, e.g., Ramos v. Holder, 589 F.3d 426 (7th Cir. 2009).

[110] See, e.g., Henriquez-Rivas v. Holder, 707 F.3d 1081 (9th Cir. 2013).

[111] See, e.g., Perez-Perez v. Holder, No. 13-1711, 2014 U.S. App. LEXIS 8786 (4th Cir., May 9, 2014).

[112] Compare Ulloa Santos v. Attorney General, 552 Fed. App'x 197 (3d Cir. 2014) ("[T]he group appears to have been defined principally, if not exclusively, for purposes of this asylum case.") (internal citation and quotations omitted) with Olmos Borja v. Holder, 550 Fed. App'x 517, 519 (9th Cir. 2013) (finding the alien eligible for asylum).

[113] See, e.g., Flores Munoz, 2014 U.S. App. LEXIS 8974, at *2 ("Though [the applicant] testified that members of a drug gang who killed her husband sought to recruit her to sell drugs for them and that she feared for her life because she turned down their requests, the evidence that she put forward does not compel the conclusion that Honduran 26 I. & N. Dec. 208, 222 (2014) ("scant evidence" produced by the applicant seen as insufficient). Significantly, in February 2014, the BIA rephrased the test for the cognizability of alleged social groups from one focused on "social visibility" to one focused on "social distinction". See Matter of W-G-R-, 26 I. & N. Dec. 208 (2014); Matter of M-E-V-G-, 26 I. & N. Dec. 227 (2014). It remains to be seen how this change may affect applications for asylum, including on gang-related grounds, although some commentators have suggested that the new standard, if upheld by the federal courts of appeals, could make it more difficult for asylum applicants to prove their cases. See, e.g., Pirir-Boc, 2014 U.S. App. LEXIS 8577, at *22 (noting that the meaning of the term particular social group is "in flux, and it is premature to determine precisely how the rule [articulated in the BIA's recent decisions] will be implemented"); Ashley Huebner & Lisa Koop, New BIA Decisions Undermine U.S. Obligations to Protect Asylum Seekers, Nat'l Immigrant Justice Center, Feb. 18, 2014, available at http://www.immigrantjustice.org/litigation/blog/new-bia-decisions-undermine-us-obligations-protect-asylum-seekers.

[114] See, e.g., Matter of M-E-V-G-, 26 I. & N. Dec. at 251 (emphasizing that there is no "blanket rejection of all factual scenarios involving gangs," and that "[s]ocial group determinations are made on a case-by-case basis").

[115] Compare Boraj v. Holder, No. 12-4631, 2014 U.S. App. LEXIS 5013, at *4-*5 (2d Cir., Mar. 18, 2014) (applicant viewed as credible by the immigration judge) with Abrego-Centeno v. Attorney General, 552 Fed. App'x 130 (3d Cir. 2014) (applicant not seen as credible because he gave conflicting testimony).

[116] See, e.g., INA §208(b)(2)(A)(iii) (aliens as to whom there are "serious reasons" to believe that they committed a "serious nonpolitical crime" outside the United States prior to their arrival are generally ineligible for asylum).

[117] See 8 C.F.R. §208.2(b).

[118] See INA §208(b)(3)(C), 8 U.S.C. §1158(b)(3)(C); 8 C.F.R. §208.2(a).

[119] See, e.g., Ogayonne v. Mukasey, 530 F.3d 514, 519 (7th Cir. 2008); 8 C.F.R. §1208.4(a)(5)(ii).

[120] INA §208(a)(2)(B) & (D), 8 U.S.C. §1158(a)(2)(B) & (D).

[121] P.L. 110-457, §235, 122 Stat. 5074 (Dec. 23, 2008) (codified, as amended, at 8 U.S.C. §1232(c)(5)).

[122] P.L. 107-296, §462, 116 Stat. 2202 (Nov. 25, 2002) (codified, as amended, at 6 U.S.C. §279(b)(1)(A)).

[123] 8 U.S.C. §1362. See also INA §208(d)(4), 8 U.S.C. §1158(d)(4) (requiring that applicants for asylum be advised of the "privilege" of being represented by counsel and given a list of persons who can provide pro bono representation); INA §238(b)(4)(B), 8 U.S.C. §1228(b)(4)(B) (providing that aliens convicted of aggravated felonies who are subject to expedited removal under Section 238 of the INA shall "have the privilege of being represented (at no expense to the government) by such counsel ... as the alien shall choose"); INA §240(a)(1)(E), 8 U.S.C. §1229a(a)(1)(E) (aliens placed in formal removal proceedings are to be given written notice that they may be represented by counsel); INA §240(b)(4)(A), 8 U.S.C. §1229a(b)(4)(A) (aliens in removal proceedings have right to counsel at no expense to the government).

[124] See, e.g., Gonzalez Machado v. Ashcroft, Order Granting Motion to Dismiss, No. CS-01-0066-FVS (E.D. Wash. June 18, 2002) (copy on file with the authors); Perez-Funez v. District Director, 619 F. Supp. 656 (C.D. Cal. 1985).

[125] For further discussion of the other types of civil proceedings in which children have been found to have a categorical right to counsel at government expense, and the ways in which such proceedings may be distinguishable from removal proceedings, see generally CRS Report R43613, Aliens' Right to Counsel in Removal Proceedings: In Brief, by Kate M. Manuel, at notes 60-64 and accompanying text.

[126] See Aguilera-Enriquez v. INS, 516 F.2d 565, 569 n.3 (6th Cir. 1975); Michelson v. INS, 897 F.2d 465, 468 (10th Cir. 1990); Ruiz v. INS, 787 F.2d 1294, 1297 n.3 (9th Cir. 1996); Barthold v. INS, 517 F.2d 689, 690-691 (5th Cir. 1975).

[127] Cf. Wade v. Mayo, 334 U.S. 672, 683-684 (1948) ("There are some individuals who, by reason of age, ignorance, or mental capacity, are incapable of representing themselves in a prosecution of a relatively simple nature. ... Where such incapacity is present, the refusal to appoint counsel is a denial of due process of law.").

[128] Franco-Gonzales v. Holder, 767 F. Supp. 2d 1034 (C.D. Cal. 2010). In response to the district court's decision in Franco-Gonzales, DOJ and DHS adopted a "nationwide policy" regarding unrepresented immigration detainees with "serious mental disorders or conditions that may render them mentally incompetent to represent themselves in immigration proceedings." Among other things, this policy calls for procedures that would make "qualified representatives"—a term which includes, but is not limited to licensed attorneys—available to such individuals at the government's expense or on a pro bono basis. Dep't of Justice, Press Release, Department of Justice and the Department of Homeland Security Announce Safeguards for Unrepresented Immigration Detainees with Serious Mental Disorders or Conditions, Apr. 22, 2013, available at http://www. justice.gov/eoir/press/2013/ SafeguardsUnrepresentedImmigrationDetainees.html.

[129] See, e.g., Kirk Semple, Youths Facing Deportation To Be Given Legal Counsel, N.Y. TIMES, June 6, 2014, available at http://www.nytimes.com/2014/06/07/us/us-to-provide-lawyers-for-children-facing-deportation.html?_r=0.

[130] See 8 U.S.C. §1362.

[131] See, e.g., Escobar Ruiz v. INS, 787 F.2d 1294 (9th Cir. 1986) (rejecting the argument that Section 292 of the INA bars the payment of attorney fees, pursuant to the Equal Access to Justice Act (EAJA), to prevailing plaintiffs); Aguilera-Enriquez, 516 F.2d at 568 (noting that the immigration judge in this case had found that Section 292 of the INA barred the provision of appointed counsel for the plaintiff); Funding of a Pilot Project for the Representation of Aliens in Immigration Proceedings, memorandum from David A. Martin, General Counsel, INS, to T. Alexander Aleinikoff, Executive Associate Commissioner, INS, Dec. 21, 1995 (reading INA §292, in conjunction with 5 U.S.C. §3106, as barring the appointment of counsel for aliens in removal proceedings) (copy on file with the authors).

[132] See Views Concerning Whether It Is Legally Permissible to Use Discretionary Funding for Representation of Aliens in Immigration Proceedings, memorandum from David A. Martin, Principal Deputy General Counsel, Department of Homeland Security, to Thomas J. Perrelli, Associate Attorney General, Department of Justice, Dec. 10, 2010 (copy on file with the authors). General principles of appropriations law could, however, potentially impose certain limitations on federal agencies' funding of counsel for aliens since appropriations may only be used for the purposes for which they were made. See generally 31 U.S.C. §1301(a) ("Appropriations shall be applied only to the objects for which the appropriations were made except as otherwise provided by law.").

[133] Vienna Convention on Consular Relations, done April 24, 1963, 21 U.S.T. 77 [hereinafter "VCCR"].

[134] Id., at art. 36.

[135] 8 C.F.R. §236.1(e). Countries with mandatory consular notification agreements are notified of the detention of one of their nationals even if the arrested aliens do not wish to have their consulate notified. Id.

[136] See State Dep't, Bureau of Consular Affairs, Countries and Jurisdictions with Mandatory Notifications, available at http://travel.state.gov/content/travel/english/ consularnotification/ countries-and-jurisdictions-with-mandatorynotifications.html (last accessed: June 26, 2014).

[137] Compare id. with CRS Report R43599, Unaccompanied Alien Children: An Overview, by Lisa Seghetti, Alison Siskin, and Ruth Ellen Wasem, at Figure 1.

[138] VCCR, at art. 5.

[139] See Betsy Cavendish & Maru Cortazar, Children at the Border: The Screening, Protection and Repatriation of Unaccompanied Mexican Minors, at 25, 46-47 (2011), available at http://appleseednetwork.org/wp-content/uploads/ 2012/05/Children-At-The-Border1.pdf.

[140] 8 C.F.R. §236.1(e).

[141] Not every pledge, assurance, or arrangement made between the United States and a foreign party constitutes a legally binding international agreement. The repatriation arrangements made between Mexico and DHS in recent years include language evidencing an intent for the arrangements not to be legally binding in nature. For background, see CRS Report RL32528, International Law and Agreements: Their Effect upon U.S. Law, by Michael John Garcia, and State Department Office of the Legal Adviser, Guidance on Non-Binding Documents, at http://www.state.gov/s/l/treaty/ guidance/.

[142] A compendium of several of these arrangements can be viewed at http://www.icc. gov/doclib/foia/repatriationagreements/el-paso-tx-local-arrangement-for-repatriation-of-mexican-nationals.pdf. A template for local arrangements between CBP or ICE field offices and Mexican Consulates General can be viewed at http://www.ice.gov/doclib/foia/ repatriation-agreements/local-arrangements-repatriation-of-mexican-nationals-full-list.pdf. The 2008 TVPRA includes a provision calling for the Secretary of State to negotiate agreements with Mexico and Canada concerning similar matters. P.L. 110-457,

§235(a)(2)(C), codified at 8 U.S.C. §1232(a)(2)(C). However, the current arrangements between local ICE and CBP offices and Mexican authorities implement DHS-Mexico arrangements that predate the 2008 TVPRA.

[143] VCCR, art. 37.

[144] Federal regulations provide that aliens granted deferred action—through DACA or upon another basis—may be granted work authorization, provided they establish an "economic necessity for employment." 8 C.F.R. §274a.12(c)(14). Because aliens granted deferred action are deemed to be lawfully present, they could potentially also be seen as eligible for certain "public benefits" whose provision to unlawfully present aliens is restricted. See CRS Legal Sidebar WSLG923, DACA Beneficiaries' Eligibility for In-State Tuition in Virginia, by Kate M. Manuel.

[145] Dep't of Homeland Security, Deferred Action for Childhood Arrivals, available at http://www.dhs.gov/deferredaction-childhood-arrivals (last accessed: June 23, 2014).

[146] Id. This reflects the standard that the Supreme Court articulated in Rosenberg v. Fleuti, 374 U.S. 449 (1963), for determining whether a return to the United States following a short absence constituted an "entry", such that the alien was subject to what were then known as the grounds of excludability.

[147] Because they are recent arrivals, UACs could potentially be classified as priorities for removal under current guidance from DHS officials regarding prosecutorial discretion. See, e.g., John Morton, then-Director, ICE, Civil Immigration Enforcement: Priorities for the Apprehension, Detention, and Removal of Aliens, Mar. 2, 2011, at 1-2, available at http://www.ice.gov/doclib/news/releases/2011/110302washingtondc.pdf (designating "recent illegal entrants" as the second priority for removal, after aliens who pose a danger to national security or a risk to public safety). However, these guidelines are not legally binding, and individual UAC could potentially have circumstances that are seen as making them a lower priority for removal (e.g., parents who have been granted Temporary Protected Status (TPS) and younger siblings who are U.S. citizens).

In: Unaccompanied Alien Children in the U.S. ISBN: 978-1-63321-832-1
Editor: Paul Snider

Chapter 4

UNAUTHORIZED ALIEN STUDENTS: ISSUES AND "DREAM ACT" LEGISLATION*

Andorra Bruno

SUMMARY

Immigration reform has been hotly debated in recent years. Broadly construed, it encompasses a range of issues, including the highly controversial question of legalizing large numbers of unauthorized immigrants in the United States. A historically less controversial, more targeted legalization proposal has been included in the "DREAM Act," legislation that seeks to enable certain unauthorized aliens who entered the United States as children to obtain legal immigration status. The name DREAM Act derives from the bill title, Development, Relief, and Education for Alien Minors Act, but it refers more broadly to measures to provide immigration relief to unauthorized students, whether or not particular bills carry that name.

Unauthorized aliens in the United States are able to receive free public education through high school. They may experience difficulty obtaining higher education, however, for several reasons. Among these reasons is a provision enacted in 1996 that prohibits states from granting unauthorized aliens certain postsecondary educational benefits on the basis of state residence, unless equal benefits are made available to all

---

* This is an edited, reformatted and augmented version of a Congressional Research Service publication, CRS Report for Congress RL33863, prepared for Members and Committees of Congress, from www.crs.gov, dated December 3, 2013.

U.S. citizens. This prohibition is commonly understood to apply to the granting of "in-state" residency status for tuition purposes. Unauthorized alien students also are not eligible for federal student financial aid. More broadly, as unauthorized aliens, they typically are not legally allowed to work and are subject to being removed from the country.

Multiple DREAM Act bills have been introduced in recent Congresses to address the unauthorized student population. Most have proposed a two-prong approach of repealing the 1996 provision and enabling some unauthorized alien students to become U.S. legal permanent residents (LPRs) through an immigration procedure known as cancellation of removal. While there are other options for dealing with this population, this report deals exclusively with the DREAM Act approach in light of the considerable congressional interest in it.

In the 111th Congress, the House approved DREAM Act language as part of an unrelated bill, the Removal Clarification Act of 2010 (H.R. 5281). The Senate, however, failed to invoke cloture on a motion to agree to the House-passed DREAM Act amendment, and the bill died at the end of the Congress. The House-approved language differed in key respects from earlier versions of the DREAM Act. Bills to legalize the status of unauthorized alien students were again introduced in the 112th Congress.

In 2012, in the absence of congressional action on DREAM Act legislation, the Obama Administration announced that certain individuals who entered the United States as children and meet other criteria would be considered for relief from removal. Under a Department of Homeland Security (DHS) memorandum, these individuals can apply for consideration of deferred action for childhood arrivals (or DACA, as the program is known). Successful applicants are granted deferred action for two years, subject to renewal, and can apply for employment authorization.

DREAM Act legislation has been considered in the 113th Congress as part of comprehensive immigration reform bills. The Senate-passed Border Security, Economic Opportunity, and Immigration Modernization Act (S. 744) includes DREAM Act provisions. The same DREAM Act language is included in a related bill with the same name introduced in the House (H.R. 15). The DREAM Act provisions are integrated with the broader legalization provisions in these bills. As of this writing, no stand-alone DREAM Act bills have been introduced in the 113th Congress.

INTRODUCTION

Immigration reform has been hotly debated in recent years. Although many component issues are controversial, the question of legalizing large numbers of unauthorized immigrants in the United States has been a focal point of debate, galvanizing both support for and opposition to reform proposals. Historically less controversial has been legislation known as the "DREAM Act" that proposes a more targeted legalization program to enable certain unauthorized students[1] to obtain legal immigration status. The name DREAM Act derives from the bill title, Development, Relief, and Education for Alien Minors Act, but it refers more broadly to measures to provide immigration relief to unauthorized alien students, whether or not particular bills carry that name.

While living in the United States, unauthorized alien children are able to receive free public education through high school.[2] Many unauthorized immigrants who graduate from high school and want to attend college, however, face various obstacles. Among them, a provision enacted in 1996 as part of the Illegal Immigration Reform and Immigrant Responsibility Act (IIRIRA)[3] discourages states and localities from granting unauthorized aliens certain "postsecondary education benefits." More broadly, as unauthorized aliens, they typically are unable to work legally and are subject to removal from the United States.[4]

Multiple bills have been introduced in recent Congresses to provide relief to unauthorized aliens who were brought into the United States as children. Prior to the 111th Congress, DREAM Act bills generally proposed to repeal the 1996 provision and to enable certain unauthorized alien students to adjust to legal permanent resident (LPR) status.[5] In the 111th Congress, the House approved a different type of DREAM Act measure as an amendment to an unrelated bill (H.R. 5281). Unlike earlier DREAM Act bills, the DREAM Act language added to H.R. 5281 did not include a repeal of the 1996 provision and proposed to grant eligible individuals an interim legal status prior to enabling them to adjust to LPR status. H.R. 5281 died at the end of the 111th Congress.

Bills to legalize the status of unauthorized alien students were again introduced in the 112th Congress. Some of these bills were similar to the measure approved by the House in the 111th Congress, while others included more traditional DREAM Act elements. In the 113th Congress, DREAM Act provisions are included in larger comprehensive immigration reform bills and are integrated with other legalization provisions in these bills.

HIGHER EDUCATION BENEFITS AND IMMIGRATION STATUS

Under federal law, unauthorized aliens are neither entitled to nor prohibited from admission to postsecondary educational institutions in the United States. State laws vary and may prohibit enrollment in public postsecondary institutions. To gain entrance to available institutions, unauthorized aliens must meet the same requirements as any other student, which vary depending on the institution and may include possessing a high school diploma, passing entrance exams, and surpassing a high school grade point average (GPA) threshold. Although admissions applications for most colleges and universities request that students provide their Social Security numbers, this information typically is not required for admission.

Even if they are able to gain admission, however, unauthorized alien students often find it difficult, if not impossible, to pay for higher education. Under the Higher Education Act (HEA) of 1965, as amended, they are ineligible for federal financial aid.[6] In most instances, unauthorized alien students are likewise ineligible for state financial aid. Furthermore, as explained in the next section, they also may be ineligible for in-state tuition rates.

1996 PROVISION

Section 505 of IIRIRA places restrictions on state provision of educational benefits to unauthorized aliens. It directs that an unauthorized alien

> shall not be eligible on the basis of residence within a State (or a political subdivision) for any postsecondary education benefit unless a citizen or national of the United States is eligible for such a benefit (in no less an amount, duration, and scope) without regard to whether the citizen or national is such a resident.

There is disagreement about the meaning of this provision, and no authoritative guidance is available in either congressional report language or federal regulations.[7] The conference report on the bill containing IIRIRA did not explain Section 505. (A conference report on a predecessor IIRIRA bill, which contained a section identical to Section 505, described the section as "provid[ing] that illegal aliens are not eligible for in-state tuition rates at public institutions of higher education.")[8] Some observers have argued that Congress exceeded its authority in Section 505 by legislating on how states can dispense state benefits.[9]

Although Section 505 does not refer explicitly to the granting of "in-state" residency status for tuition purposes and some question whether it even covers in-state tuition, the debate surrounding Section 505 has focused on the provision of in-state tuition rates to unauthorized aliens. A key issue in this debate is whether it is possible to grant in-state tuition to resident unauthorized students (and not to all citizens) without violating Section 505. Various states have attempted to do this. For example, a California law passed in 2001 makes unauthorized aliens eligible for instate tuition at state community colleges and California State University campuses.[10] The measure, however, bases eligibility on criteria that do not explicitly include state residency. The requirements to qualify for in-state tuition under the California law include attendance at a California high school for at least three years and either graduation from a California high school "or attainment of the equivalent thereof." In addition, the law requires an unauthorized alien student to file an affidavit stating that he or she either has filed an application to legalize his or her status or will file such an application as soon as he or she is eligible. California officials have argued that by using eligibility criteria other than state residency, the law does not violate the Section 505 prohibition on conferring educational benefits on the basis of state residency. In November 2010, the California Supreme Court upheld the California law. At least one federal court also has considered whether state laws that authorize in-state tuition for unauthorized students violate Section 505.[11]

DEFERRED ACTION FOR CHILDHOOD ARRIVALS (DACA)

On June 15, 2012, in the absence of congressional action on DREAM Act bills, the Department of Homeland Security (DHS) issued a memorandum[12] announcing that certain individuals who were brought to the United States as children and meet other criteria would be considered for deferred action[13] for two years, subject to renewal. The eligibility criteria for deferred action for childhood arrivals, or DACA, as the initiative is known, are similar to those for relief in DREAM Act bills. These criteria include the following: (1) under age 16 at time of entry into the United States; (2) continuous residence in the United States for at least five years before June 15, 2012 (that is, since June 15, 2007); (3) in school, graduated from high school or obtained general education development certificate, or honorably discharged from the Armed Forces; (4) not convicted of a felony, a significant misdemeanor, or three or more misdemeanors, and not otherwise a threat to national security or public safety; and (5) age 30 or below on June 15, 2012. Consideration for DACA is limited to individuals who entered the United States without inspection or whose lawful immigration status expired as of June 15, 2012. Aliens granted deferred action can apply for employment authorization. The DACA program, however, provides no pathway to a legal immigration status.14 DHS began accepting requests for consideration of deferred action for childhood arrivals in August 2012.

ESTIMATES OF POTENTIAL DREAM ACT BENEFICIARIES

Traditional DREAM Act bills would enable certain unauthorized alien students to obtain LPR status in the United States through a two-stage process. Requirements to obtain conditional status (stage 1) typically include residence of at least five years in the United States, and a high school diploma (or the equivalent) or admission to an institution of higher education in the United States. Requirements to become a full-fledged LPR (stage 2) typically include acquisition of a degree from an institution of higher education in the United States, completion of at least two years in a bachelor's or higher degree program, or service in the uniformed services for at least two years.

In 2010, using data from the March 2006, March 2007, and March 2008 Current Population Survey (CPS) and other sources, the Migration Policy Institute (MPI) published estimates of the population potentially eligible for legal status under S. 729, a Senate DREAM Act bill introduced in the 111th Congress.[15] This bill would have established a two-stage process for unauthorized alien students to obtain LPR status. Aliens who met specified age, physical presence, educational, and other requirements could have first applied for conditional LPR status. After meeting additional requirements, including two years of either college or service in the uniformed services, they could have applied to have the condition on their status removed and become full-fledged LPRs.[16]

According to the MPI analysis, if this DREAM Act bill had been enacted, about 2.150 million individuals could have attempted to become LPRs under its provisions. This total included estimates of individuals who, on the date of enactment, would already have met the substantive requirements under the bill for conditional status (or for both conditional status and the removal of the condition), as well as estimates of individuals who, on the date of enactment, would have met some, but not all, of the requirements for conditional status. About 43% (934,000) of the estimated 2.150 million potential beneficiaries were children under age 18 in elementary or secondary school. The MPI report also included an estimate of the number of individuals who likely would have obtained LPR status under S. 729, if it had been enacted:

> If future behavior mirrors past trends, we project that approximately 38 percent [of the 2.15 million]—or 825,000—of the potential beneficiaries would actually achieve lawful permanent status under the legislation.[17]

As part of a 2010 analysis of the costs and likely impact of DREAM Act legislation before the 111th Congress, the Center for Immigration Studies (CIS) similarly estimated the number of potential DREAM Act beneficiaries using 2009 and 2010 CPS data.[18] Although CIS did not identify the bills at issue in its analysis, the bill requirements mentioned matched those in S. 729, as described above, and S. 3827, a similar bill introduced in the 111th Congress.[19] CIS estimated that there were some 1.998 million unauthorized aliens who would have met the residency and age requirements under the DREAM Act legislation, including 859,000 children under age 18. Of the 1.998 million potential beneficiaries, CIS estimated that 1.426 million individuals would have met the high school graduation, or equivalent, requirement for conditional LPR status (either on the date of enactment or at a later date). CIS, however, did not provide an estimate of the number of individuals who likely would have obtained LPR status under the DREAM Act.

Estimates of Potential DACA Beneficiaries

In August 2012, MPI produced estimates of the potentially eligible population under DHS's deferred action for childhood arrivals policy based on guidelines issued by the agency. MPI estimated that as many as 1.8 million unauthorized aliens in the United States could be eligible for DACA relief.[20] As of August 31, 2013, a total of 455,455 requests for consideration of DACA had been approved.[21]

ACTION IN THE 112TH CONGRESS

Similar, but not identical, Senate and House DREAM Act bills (S. 952, H.R. 1842) were introduced in the 112th Congress. Although there were differences between the bills, both were entitled the Development, Relief, and Education for Alien Minors (DREAM) Act of 2011. Both likewise took a step back from some of the revisions incorporated in the DREAM Act measure approved by the House in the 111th Congress[22] and included some more traditional DREAM Act provisions. By contrast, other House bills (H.R. 3823, H.R. 5869) more closely resembled the version of the DREAM Act approved by the House in 2010.

S. 952

S. 952, the DREAM Act of 2011, was introduced by Senator Richard Durbin with 32 original cosponsors. It would have repealed IIRIRA Section 505 and thereby eliminated this statutory restriction on state provision of postsecondary educational benefits to unauthorized aliens. It also would have enabled eligible unauthorized students (including those in temporary protected status under the Immigration and Nationality Act (INA))[23] to adjust to LPR status in the United States through an immigration procedure known as cancellation of removal. Cancellation of removal is a discretionary form of relief that an alien can apply for while in removal proceedings before an immigration judge. If cancellation of removal is granted in removal proceedings, the alien's status is adjusted to that of an LPR. S. 952 would have enabled aliens to affirmatively apply for cancellation of removal without first being placed in removal proceedings, and it would have placed no limit on the number of aliens who could be granted cancellation of removal/adjustment of status under its provisions.

To be eligible for cancellation of removal/adjustment of status under S. 952, an alien would have had to demonstrate that he or she had been continuously physically present in the United States for five years immediately preceding the date of enactment of the act; was age 15 or younger at the time of initial entry; had been a person of good moral character since the time of initial entry; and was age 35 or younger on the date of enactment. The alien also would have needed to demonstrate that he or she had been admitted to an institution of higher education in the United States or had earned a high school diploma or the equivalent in the United States.

Aliens applying for relief under S. 952 would have been subject to special requirements concerning inadmissibility. The INA enumerates classes of inadmissible aliens. Under the INA, except as otherwise provided, aliens who are inadmissible under specified grounds, such as health-related grounds or criminal grounds, are ineligible to receive visas from the Department of State or to be admitted to the United States by the Department of Homeland Security.[24] S. 952 would have specified the grounds of inadmissibility applicable to aliens seeking relief.[25] An alien applying for cancellation of removal/adjustment of status under S. 952 would have had to show that he or she was not inadmissible on INA criminal, security, smuggling, student visa abuse, citizenship ineligibility, polygamy, international child abduction, or unlawful voting grounds.[26] Applicants also would have needed to satisfy requirements concerning convictions for offenses under federal or state law. In addition, they would have had to submit biometric and biographic data, which would have been used to conduct background checks, and would have needed to register under the Military Selective Service Act, if applicable.

S. 952 would have required that applications for cancellation of removal/adjustment of status be filed not later than one year after the date the alien earned a high school diploma or the equivalent, or the effective date of final regulations, whichever was later. Under the bill, the Secretary of Homeland Security or the Attorney General could not have removed an alien with a pending application who established prima facie eligibility for relief. In addition, the Attorney General would have stayed the removal proceedings of an alien who was at least age five,[27] met all the eligibility requirements except high school graduation, and was enrolled in primary or secondary school.

Aliens granted cancellation of removal under S. 952 would have been adjusted initially to *conditional* permanent resident status. Such conditional status would have been valid for six years and would have been subject to termination. To have the condition removed and become a full-fledged LPR, an alien would have had to submit an application during a specified period and meet additional requirements. Among these requirements, the alien would have needed to have demonstrated good moral character during the period of conditional permanent residence; could not have abandoned his or her U.S. residence; and would have needed either to have earned a degree from an institution of higher education (or to have completed at least two years in a bachelor's or higher degree program) in the United States or to have served in the uniformed services[28] for at least two years. Other requirements for removal of the condition would have included satisfaction of the English language and civics requirements for naturalization, submission of biometric and biographic data, and completion of background checks.

S. 952 would have placed restrictions on the eligibility of aliens who had conditional LPR status under the bill for federal student financial aid under Title IV of the Higher Education Act of 1965, as amended (see "Higher Education Benefits and Immigration Status"). Aliens with conditional LPR status would have been eligible only for student loans, federal work-study programs, and services (such as counseling, tutorial services, and mentoring), subject to the applicable requirements. They would have been ineligible for federal Pell Grants or federal supplemental educational opportunity grants.

The time an alien spent as a conditional LPR would have counted for naturalization[29] purposes under S. 952. (Typically, an alien must be in LPR status for five years before he or she can naturalize.) Under S. 952, however, the condition on the LPR status would have had to have been removed before an alien could apply for naturalization.

H.R. 1842

H.R. 1842, the DREAM Act of 2011, was introduced by Representative Howard Berman with bipartisan cosponsorship. It was similar in many respects to S. 952, but different in some areas. Like the Senate bill, it would have repealed IIRIRA Section 505 and thereby eliminated this restriction on state provision of postsecondary educational benefits to unauthorized aliens. It also would have enabled eligible unauthorized students to adjust to LPR status in the United States through cancellation of removal. Unlike S. 952, it would not have provided for adjustment to LPR status for aliens in temporary protected status. Like S. 952, it would have enabled aliens to affirmatively apply for cancellation of removal without first being placed in removal proceedings, and it would have placed no limit on the number of aliens who could be granted cancellation of removal/adjustment of status.

H.R. 1842 included many of the same requirements as S. 952 for cancellation of removal/ adjustment of status. Under the House bill, as under the Senate bill, an alien would have needed to demonstrate that he or she had been continuously physically present in the United States for not less than five years immediately preceding the date of enactment of the act; was age 15 or younger at the time of initial entry; had been a person of good moral character since the time of initial entry; and had been admitted to an institution of higher education in the United States or had earned a high school diploma or the equivalent in the United States. Under H.R. 1842, the alien would have needed to demonstrate that he or she was age 32 or younger on the date of enactment, compared to age 35 or younger under the Senate bill.

With respect to the INA grounds of inadmissibility, an alien applying for relief under H.R. 1842, as under S. 952, would have had to show that he or she was not inadmissible on INA criminal, security, smuggling, student visa abuse, citizenship ineligibility, polygamy, international child abduction, or unlawful voting grounds.[30] An additional ground of inadmissibility—the public charge ground (i.e., indigence)—would have applied under the House bill. As under S. 952, applicants for relief under H.R. 1842 would have had to submit biometric and biographic data, which would have been used to conduct background checks, and would have needed to register under the Military Selective Service Act, if applicable. They would not have been subject to requirements like those in S. 952 related to convictions for offenses under federal or state law.

The provisions in H.R. 1842 concerning the application process and protection from removal for potential beneficiaries were very similar to those in S. 952. Like S. 952, the House bill would have required that applications be filed not later than one year after the date the alien earned a high school diploma or the equivalent, or the effective date of final regulations, whichever was later. Under the House bill, the Secretary of Homeland Security or the Attorney General could not have removed an alien with a pending application who established prima facie eligibility for relief. In addition, the Attorney General would have stayed the removal proceedings of an alien who was at least age 12 (compared to the age five cutoff in S. 952), met all the eligibility requirements except high school graduation, and was enrolled in primary or secondary school.

Aliens granted cancellation of removal under H.R. 1842, as under S. 952, would have been adjusted initially to conditional permanent resident status. Such conditional status would have been valid for six years and would have been subject to termination. To have the condition removed and become a full-fledged LPR, an alien would have had to submit an application during a specified period and meet additional requirements. Among these requirements, the alien would have needed to have demonstrated good moral character during the period of conditional permanent residence; could not have abandoned his or her U.S. residence; and would have needed either to have earned a degree from an institution of higher education (or to have completed at least two years in a bachelor's or higher degree program) in the United States or to have served in the uniformed services for at least two years. Other requirements for removal of the condition would have included satisfaction of the English language and civics requirements for naturalization, submission of biometric and biographic data, and completion of background checks. The time an alien spent as a conditional LPR would have counted for naturalization purposes under H.R. 1842, but the condition on the LPR status would have had to be removed before an alien could apply for naturalization.

H.R. 1842 would have placed temporary restrictions on the eligibility of aliens who adjusted to LPR status under its provisions for federal student financial aid under Title IV of the Higher Education Act of 1965, as amended. Aliens adjusting status under the bill who were in conditional permanent resident status would have been eligible for student loans, federal work-study programs, and services, but they would not have been eligible for federal Pell Grants and federal supplemental educational opportunity grants.

H.R. 3823

H.R. 3823, the Adjusted Residency for Military Service (ARMS) Act, was introduced by Representative David Rivera. It was similar in many respects to the DREAM Act language approved by the House as part of H.R. 5281 in the 111th Congress,[31] and it was significantly different than S. 952 and H.R. 1842. Unlike S. 952 and H.R. 1842, H.R. 3823 would not have repealed IIRIRA Section 505 and thus would not have eliminated this statutory restriction on state provision of postsecondary educational benefits to unauthorized aliens. Unlike S. 952, H.R. 1842, and the House-approved measure in the 111th Congress, H.R. 3823 would have required unauthorized alien students to perform military service in order to obtain LPR status.

Under H.R. 3823, as under the House-approved DREAM Act language in the 111th Congress, an eligible alien could have gone through the cancellation of removal procedure and been granted conditional *nonimmigrant* status. Unlike under S. 952, H.R. 1842, and most other DREAM Act bills introduced in past Congresses, the alien's status would not have been adjusted to that of a conditional LPR.

Like most other DREAM Act bills, H.R. 3823 would have enabled an alien to affirmatively apply for cancellation of removal without first being placed in removal proceedings; would have established a deadline for submitting initial cancellation of removal applications; and would have prohibited the Secretary of Homeland Security from removing an alien with a pending application who established prima facie eligibility for relief. Unlike other DREAM Act bills, H.R. 3823 did not include provisions about staying the removal proceedings of alien children who were enrolled in primary or secondary school and who met all the eligibility requirements for initial conditional status except high school graduation.

To be eligible for cancellation of removal/conditional nonimmigrant status under H.R. 3823, an alien would have needed to demonstrate that he or she: had been physically present in the United States for a continuous period of not less than five years immediately preceding the date of enactment of the legislation; had not yet reached age 16 at the time of initial entry; had been a person of good moral character since the date of initial entry; and was younger than age 30 on the date of enactment. These requirements were the same as in S. 952 and H.R. 1842, except for the maximum age limitation on the date of enactment.[32] Under H.R. 3823, the alien also would have had to demonstrate that he or she had been admitted to an institution of higher education in the United States, or had earned a high school diploma or the equivalent in the United States, as under both S. 952 and H.R. 1842, and that he or she had never been under a final administrative or judicial order of exclusion, deportation, or removal, with some exceptions.

H.R. 3823 specified the grounds of inadmissibility and deportability that would have applied to aliens seeking relief. An alien applying for cancellation of removal/conditional nonimmigrant status under the bill would have had to show that he or she was not inadmissible on INA health-related, criminal, security, public charge, smuggling, student visa abuse, citizenship ineligibility, polygamy, international child abduction, or unlawful voting grounds, and was not deportable on INA criminal, security, smuggling, marriage fraud, public charge, or unlawful voting grounds.[33] Applicants also would have needed to satisfy requirements concerning convictions for offenses under federal or state law. In addition, they would have had to submit biometric and biographic data, which would have been used to conduct background checks, and would have needed to register under the Military Selective Service Act, if applicable.

As noted above, an alien whose removal was cancelled under H.R. 3823 would have been granted conditional nonimmigrant status, as opposed to conditional LPR status under S. 952 and H.R. 1842. Such conditional nonimmigrant status would have been valid for an initial period of five years and would have been subject to termination. Among the grounds for termination would have been failure to successfully enlist in the Armed Forces[34] within nine months after being granted conditional status.

Under H.R. 3823, an alien's conditional nonimmigrant status would have been extended for a second five-year period (for a total conditional period of

10 years) if the alien met the following requirements: demonstration of good moral character as a conditional nonimmigrant; compliance with the bill's inadmissibility and deportability provisions discussed above; no abandonment of U.S. residence; and service in the Armed Forces on active duty for at least two years or service in a reserve component of the Armed Forces in active status for at least four years.

By comparison, under the House-approved measure in the 111th Congress, there also would have been two five-year conditional nonimmigrant status periods and beneficiaries would have had to meet a set of requirements to have their status extended for the second five-year period. With respect to the requirements for extension, however, the House-approved measure included different military service requirements than H.R. 3823 and, unlike that bill, would have given beneficiaries the option of completing two years of higher education instead of serving in the Armed Forces.

Another similarity to the DREAM Act language approved in the 111th Congress, and a difference from S. 952, H.R. 1842, and other DREAM Act bills, was that H.R. 3823 would have established surcharges on applications for relief. There would have been a surcharge of $525 on each application for cancellation of removal/conditional nonimmigrant status, and a surcharge of $2,000 on each application for an extension of conditional nonimmigrant status.

At the end of the second period of conditional nonimmigrant status, as specified, the alien could have applied for adjustment to LPR status. Among the requirements for adjustment of status, the alien would have needed to have demonstrated good moral character during the period of conditional nonimmigrant status; would have needed to be in compliance with the bill's inadmissibility and deportability provisions; and could not have abandoned his or her U.S. residence. In addition, applicants for adjustment of status under H.R. 3823, as under the House-approved version of the DREAM Act in the 111th Congress, would have needed to satisfy the English language and civic requirements for naturalization, satisfy any applicable federal tax liability, submit biometric and biographic data, and complete background checks. There would have been no limitation on the number of individuals eligible for adjustment of status.

Under H.R. 3823, aliens who adjusted status and met other requirements would have been eligible for naturalization after three years in LPR status. Unlike under S. 952 and H.R. 1842, the time spent in conditional status under H.R. 3823 (during which the aliens would have been conditional nonimmigrants) would not have counted for naturalization purposes.

H.R. 3823 also contained provisions on the treatment for other purposes of aliens who were granted conditional nonimmigrant status or LPR status under the bill. Like the version of the DREAM Act approved by the 111th Congress, H.R. 3823 would have directed that conditional nonimmigrants be considered lawfully present for all purposes except for provisions in the Patient Protection and Affordable Care Act (PPACA), as enacted by the 111th Congress,[35] concerning premium tax credits and cost sharing subsidies.[36] It also would have directed that aliens who adjusted to LPR status under the bill be deemed to have completed the five-year period required for LPR eligibility for certain types of federal public assistance, as established by the Personal Responsibility and Work Opportunity Reconciliation Act (PRWORA) of 1996.[37] H.R. 3823 contained no provisions on the eligibility of aliens who were granted relief under its provisions for federal student financial aid.

H.R. 5869

H.R. 5869, the Studying Towards Adjusted Residency Status (STARS) Act, was also introduced by Representative Rivera. It was a counterpart bill to H.R. 3823 (discussed above) in that it would have provided a pathway to LPR status through higher education, while H.R. 3823 would have provided a pathway through military service. H.R. 5869, like H.R. 3823, was similar in many respects to the DREAM Act language approved by the House as part of H.R. 5281 in the 111th Congress,[38] and it was significantly different than S. 952 and H.R. 1842. Like H.R. 3823 and the DREAM Act language approved by the House in the 111th Congress, H.R. 5869 would not have repealed IIRIRA Section 505 and thus would not have eliminated this statutory restriction on state provision of postsecondary educational benefits to unauthorized aliens.

Under H.R. 5869, as under H.R. 3823 and the House-approved DREAM Act language in the 111th Congress, an eligible alien could have gone through the cancellation of removal procedure and been granted conditional nonimmigrant status. Unlike under S. 952, H.R. 1842, and most other DREAM Act bills introduced in past Congresses, the alien's status would not have been adjusted to that of a conditional LPR.

Like most other DREAM Act bills, H.R. 5869 would have enabled an alien to affirmatively apply for cancellation of removal without first being placed in removal proceedings and would have prohibited the Secretary of Homeland Security from removing an alien with a pending application who established prima facie eligibility for relief. Unlike some other DREAM Act bills, H.R. 5869 did not include provisions about staying the removal proceedings of alien children who were enrolled in primary or secondary school and who met all the eligibility requirements for initial conditional status except high school graduation.

To be eligible for cancellation of removal/conditional nonimmigrant status under H.R. 5869, an alien would have had to demonstrate that he or she had been physically present in the United States for a continuous period of not less than five years immediately preceding the date of enactment of the legislation; had not yet reached age 16 at the time of initial entry; had been a person of good moral character since the date of initial entry; and was younger than age 30 on the date of enactment. These requirements were the same as in S. 952 and H.R. 1842, except for the maximum age limitation on the date of enactment.[39]

The educational requirements for conditional status in H.R. 5869, however, were different than in S. 952 and H.R. 1842 and in other traditional DREAM Act bills. Under H.R. 5869, the applicant would have had to demonstrate that he or she had earned a high school diploma or the equivalent in the United States, *and* had been admitted to an *accredited four-year* institution of higher education in the United States. In addition, as under H.R. 3823, the alien would have had to demonstrate that he or she had never been under a final administrative or judicial order of exclusion, deportation, or removal, with some exceptions.

H.R. 5869 specified the grounds of inadmissibility and deportability that would have applied to aliens seeking relief. They were the same grounds as under H.R. 3823. An alien applying for cancellation of removal/conditional nonimmigrant status under H.R. 5869 would have to show that he or she was not inadmissible on INA health-related, criminal, security, public charge, smuggling, student visa abuse, citizenship ineligibility, polygamy, international child abduction, or unlawful voting grounds, and was not deportable on INA criminal, security, smuggling, marriage fraud, public charge, or unlawful voting grounds.[40] Applicants also would have needed to satisfy requirements concerning convictions for offenses under federal or state law. In addition, they would have had to submit biometric and biographic data, which would have been used to conduct background checks, and they would have needed to register under the Military Selective Service Act, if applicable.

An alien whose removal was cancelled under H.R. 5869 would have been granted conditional nonimmigrant status, as opposed to conditional LPR status under traditional DREAM Act bills.

Such conditional nonimmigrant status would have been valid for an initial period of five years and would have been subject to termination. Among the grounds for termination would have been failure to enroll in an accredited four-year institution within one year after being granted conditional status or failure to remain enrolled in such an institution.

Under H.R. 5869, an alien's conditional nonimmigrant status would have been extended for a second five-year period (for a total conditional period of 10 years) if the alien met the following requirements: demonstration of good moral character as a conditional nonimmigrant; compliance with the bill's inadmissibility and deportability provisions discussed above; no abandonment of U.S. residence; and graduation from an accredited four-year institution of higher education in the United States.

Like H.R. 3823, H.R. 5869 would have established surcharges on applications for relief. There would have been a surcharge of $525 on each application for cancellation of removal/conditional nonimmigrant status, and a surcharge of $2,000 on each application for an extension of conditional nonimmigrant status.

At the end of the second period of conditional nonimmigrant status, as specified, the alien could have applied for adjustment to LPR status. Among the requirements for adjustment of status were demonstration of good moral character during the period of conditional nonimmigrant status, compliance with the bill's inadmissibility and deportability provisions, and no abandonment of the alien's U.S. residence. In addition, applicants for adjustment of status under H.R. 5869 would have needed to satisfy the English language and civic requirements for naturalization, satisfy any applicable federal tax liability, submit biometric and biographic data, and complete background checks. There would have been no limitation on the number of individuals eligible for adjustment of status. Under H.R. 5869, as under H.R. 3823, aliens who adjusted status and met other requirements would have been eligible for naturalization after three years in LPR status.

H.R. 5869 also contained provisions on the treatment for other purposes of aliens granted conditional nonimmigrant status or LPR status under the bill. Like the version of the DREAM Act approved by the House in the 111th Congress and H.R. 3823, H.R. 5869 would have provided that conditional nonimmigrants were to be considered lawfully present for all purposes except for provisions in the Patient Protection and Affordable Care Act concerning premium tax credits and cost sharing subsidies. It also would have directed that aliens who adjusted to LPR status under the bill be deemed to have completed the five-year period required for LPR eligibility for certain types of federal public assistance, as established by the Personal Responsibility and Work Opportunity Reconciliation Act of 1996. Unlike other DREAM Act bills that offered a higher education route to LPR status, H.R. 5869 contained no provisions on the eligibility of aliens who were granted relief under its provisions for federal student financial aid.

ACTION IN THE 113TH CONGRESS

In the 113th Congress, DREAM Act provisions have been incorporated into larger comprehensive immigration reform bills. Both the Border Security, Economic Opportunity, and Immigration Modernization Act (S. 744), as passed by the Senate,[41] and a related House bill of the same name (H.R. 15), as introduced in the House, include the same DREAM Act language. As of this writing, no stand-alone DREAM Act bills have been introduced in the 113th Congress.

S. 744 and H.R. 15 propose to establish a general legalization program for unauthorized aliens in the United States, with a special "DREAM Act" pathway to LPR status for certain aliens who entered the country as children.[42] Both bills would establish a new multi-step, multi-year process for eligible unauthorized aliens to transition into a provisional legal status and ultimately to lawful permanent residence. They would add a new section (245B) to the INA, providing for adjustment to a newly created *registered provisional immigrant (RPI)* status. The Secretary of Homeland Security would be authorized to grant RPI status to a foreign national who meets the specified eligibility requirements, submits an application in the specified period, and pays a fee and a penalty, if applicable.[43] Under S. 744 and H.R. 15, the initial period of RPI status would be six years, which could be extended if the alien remains eligible for RPI status and meets specified requirements.

The RPI eligibility requirements in S. 744 and H.R. 15 state that the alien: must be physically present in the United States on the date of submitting the RPI application; must have been physically present in the United States on or before December 31, 2011; and must have maintained continuous physical presence in the United States from December 31, 2011, until the date the alien is granted RPI status. Dependent spouses and children could be classified as RPI dependents if they were physically present in the United States on or before December 31, 2012; have maintained continuous physical presence in the United States from that date until the date the principal alien is granted RPI status; and meet the other RPI eligibility requirements.

Under S. 744 and H.R. 15, a foreign national would be ineligible for RPI status: if he or she has a conviction for specified criminal offenses or for unlawful voting; if the Secretary of Homeland Security knows or has reasonable grounds to believe that the alien has engaged, or is likely to engage, in terrorist activity; or if the alien is inadmissible under specified INA grounds, including health-related, criminal, security, smuggling, citizenship ineligibility, polygamy, international child abduction, unlawful voting, and renunciation of U.S. citizenship to avoid taxation grounds.[44] Aliens with LPR, refugee, asylum, or (with specified exceptions) legal nonimmigrant status on the date S. 744 was introduced also would be ineligible.

Aliens seeking RPI status under S. 744 or H.R. 15 would be required to pay both a processing fee and a penalty, but the penalty fee would not apply to individuals who meet the DREAM Act criteria described below. The bills would further require that aliens satisfy any applicable federal tax liability prior to filing an RPI application, and that aliens submit biometric and biographic data and clear national security and law enforcement background checks as part of the application process. An RPI applicant also could be subject to additional security screening at the discretion of the DHS Secretary. An alien granted RPI status or who appears prima facie eligible for RPI status would be provided with specified protections from removal under S. 744 and H.R. 15.[45]

S. 744 and H.R. 15 would further amend the INA[46] to establish a special pathway to LPR status for RPIs who entered the United States as children and satisfy a set of requirements similar to those traditionally included in DREAM Act bills. Under these provisions, the DHS Secretary could adjust the status of an RPI to that of an LPR if the alien demonstrates that he or she: has been an RPI for at least five years; was under age 16 at the time of initial entry into the United States; has earned a high school diploma, general education development (GED) certificate, or the equivalent in the United States; and has earned a degree from an institution of higher education or has completed at least two years in good standing in a bachelor's or higher degree program in the United States, or has served in the uniformed services for at least four years. Such aliens would be subject to English language and civics requirements and to national security and law enforcement screening. RPIs adjusting to LPR status under the DREAM Act provisions, however, would be exempt from the $1,000 penalty applicable to RPIs adjusting status under other provisions. There would be no limit on the number of aliens who could adjust status under the DREAM Act provisions in S. 744 and H.R. 15.

S. 744 and H.R. 15 include language on federal student assistance under Title IV of the Higher Education Act (see "Higher Education Benefits and Immigration Status") for RPIs who initially entered the United States before age 16. The bills specify that these aliens would only be eligible for student loans, federal work-study programs, and services. In addition, S. 744 and H.R. 15 would repeal Section 505 of the Illegal Immigration Reform and Immigrant Responsibility Act of 1996 (IIRIRA), which places certain restrictions on state provision of postsecondary educational benefits to unauthorized aliens (see "1996 Provision").[47]

With respect to naturalization, an alien granted LPR status under the DREAM Act provisions in S. 744 and H.R. 15 would be considered to have been lawfully admitted for permanent residence and to have been in the United States as an LPR (and therefore accumulating time toward the residency requirement for naturalization) during the period the alien was an RPI.[48] With some exceptions, however, an alien could not apply for naturalization while in RPI status.

Concluding Observations

Those who favor DREAM Act proposals to repeal Section 505 and grant LPR status to unauthorized alien students offer a variety of arguments. They maintain that it is both fair and in the U.S. national interest to enable unauthorized alien students who graduate from high school to continue their education. And they emphasize that large numbers will be unable to do so unless they are eligible for in-state tuition rates at colleges in their states of residence.

Advocates for unauthorized alien students argue that many of them were brought into the United States at a very young age and should not be held responsible for the decision to enter the country illegally. According to these advocates, many of the students have spent most of their lives in the United States and have few, if any, ties to their countries of origin. They argue that these special circumstances demand that the students be granted humanitarian relief in the form of LPR status. They further maintain that enacting the DREAM Act would have economic benefits for the United States by adding hundreds of billions of dollars to the economy and promoting new job creation.

Those who oppose making unauthorized alien students eligible for in-state tuition or legal status emphasize that the students and their families are in the

United States illegally and should be removed from the country. They object to using U.S. taxpayer money to subsidize the education of individuals (through the granting of in-state tuition rates) who are in the United States in violation of the law. They maintain that funding the education of these students should be the responsibility of their parents or their home countries. They also argue that it is unfair to charge unauthorized alien students in-state tuition while charging some U.S. citizens higher out-of-state rates.

More broadly, these opponents argue that granting benefits to unauthorized alien students rewards lawbreakers and thereby undermines the U.S. immigration system and the rule of law. Taking issue with the economic benefit argument made by DREAM Act supporters, critics maintain that the legislation would cost money and would take jobs and college spots away from legal residents and give them to people who entered the United States illegally. In their view, the availability of benefits, especially LPR status, would encourage more illegal immigration into the country.[49]

APPENDIX. ACTION IN THE 111TH CONGRESS

Many DREAM Act bills seeking to provide relief to unauthorized alien students by repealing the 1996 provision and enabling certain unauthorized alien students to obtain LPR status have been introduced in recent Congresses.[50]

Legislation in the 111th Congress

Senator Durbin and Representative Berman introduced DREAM Act bills in the 111th Congress. Senator Durbin introduced the Development, Relief, and Education for Alien Minors (DREAM) Act of 2009 (S. 729) and four versions of the Development, Relief, and Education for Alien Minors (DREAM) Act of 2010 (S. 3827, S. 3962, S. 3963, S. 3992). Representative Berman introduced the American Dream Act (H.R. 1751) and the Development, Relief, and Education for Alien Minors (DREAM) Act of 2010 (H.R. 6497). Representative Charles Djou introduced a related bill, the Citizenship and Service Act of 2010 (H.R. 6327).

On December 8, 2010, the House approved DREAM Act language as part of an unrelated bill, the Removal Clarification Act of 2010 (H.R. 5281). On December 18, 2010, the Senate failed to invoke cloture on a motion to agree to the House-passed DREAM Act amendment. The vote on the cloture motion was 55 to 41.[51]

House-Approved DREAM Act Language and H.R. 6497

The DREAM Act language approved by the House as part of H.R. 5281 was the same as the text of the DREAM Act of 2010 (H.R. 6497), as introduced by Representative Berman, and was similar to the DREAM Act of 2010 (S. 3992), as introduced by Senator Durbin. Like other DREAM Act bills in the 111th Congress, the House-approved DREAM Act amendment to H.R. 5281 would have enabled eligible unauthorized students to adjust to LPR status in the United States, although it would have established a different pathway than most of the other bills. Unlike some other DREAM Act bills introduced in the 111th Congress, the House-approved DREAM Act language would not have repealed IIRIRA Section 505 and thus would not have eliminated this statutory restriction on state provision of postsecondary educational benefits to unauthorized aliens (see "1996 Provision").

Under the House-approved DREAM Act amendment to H.R. 5281, an eligible alien could have gone through the cancellation of removal procedure and been granted conditional nonimmigrant status. Unlike under most other DREAM Act bills in the 111th Congress, as discussed below, the alien's status would not have been adjusted to that of a conditional LPR. The House-approved version of the DREAM Act would have enabled an alien to affirmatively apply for cancellation of removal without first being placed in removal proceedings and also would have established a deadline for submitting initial cancellation of removal applications.

To be eligible for cancellation of removal/conditional nonimmigrant status under the House-approved DREAM Act amendment to H.R. 5281, an alien would have needed to demonstrate that he or she: had been physically present in the United States for a continuous period of not less than five years immediately preceding the date of enactment of the legislation; had not yet reached age 16 at the time of initial entry; had been a person of good moral character since the date of initial entry; and was younger than age 30 on the date of enactment. The alien also would have had to demonstrate that he or she had been admitted to an institution of higher education in the United States or had earned a high school diploma or the equivalent in the United States; and that he or she had never been under a final administrative or judicial order of exclusion, deportation, or removal, with some exceptions.

The House-approved version of the DREAM Act specified the grounds of inadmissibility and deportability that would have applied to aliens seeking relief. An alien applying for cancellation of removal/conditional nonimmigrant status under the House-passed measure would have had to show that he or she was not inadmissible on INA health-related, criminal, security, public charge, smuggling, student visa abuse, citizenship ineligibility, polygamy, international child abduction, or unlawful voting grounds, and was not deportable on INA criminal, security, smuggling, marriage fraud, public charge, or unlawful voting grounds.[52] Applicants also would have needed to satisfy requirements concerning convictions for offenses under federal or state law. In addition, they would have had to submit biometric and biographic data, which would have been used to conduct background checks, and would have needed to register under the Military Selective Service Act, if applicable.

Aliens whose removal was cancelled under the House-approved DREAM Act amendment to H.R. 5281 would have been granted conditional nonimmigrant status. Such conditional status would have been valid for an initial period of five years and would have been subject to termination. An alien's conditional nonimmigrant status would have been extended for a second five-year period if the alien met the following requirements: demonstration of good moral character as a conditional nonimmigrant; compliance with the bill's inadmissibility and deportability provisions; no abandonment of U.S. residence; and either acquisition of a degree from an institution of higher education (or completion of at least two years in a bachelor's or higher degree program) in the United States, or service in the Armed Forces for at least two years.

Unlike other DREAM Act bills in the 111th Congress, the House-approved DREAM Act amendment to H.R. 5281 would have established surcharges on applications for relief. There would have been a surcharge of $525 on each application for cancellation of removal/conditional nonimmigrant status, and a surcharge of $2,000 on each application for an extension of conditional nonimmigrant status.

At the end of the second period of conditional nonimmigrant status, as specified, the alien could have applied for adjustment to LPR status. Among the requirements for adjustment of status, the alien would have needed to have demonstrated good moral character during the period of conditional nonimmigrant status; would have had to be in compliance with the bill's inadmissibility and deportability provisions; and could not have abandoned his or her U.S. residence. In addition, applicants for adjustment of status under the House-approved version of the DREAM Act would have needed to satisfy the English language and civic requirements for naturalization, satisfy any applicable federal tax liability, submit biometric and biographic data, and complete background checks. There would have been no limitation on the number of individuals eligible for adjustment of status.

Aliens who adjusted status and met other requirements would have been eligible for naturalization after three years in LPR status. Unlike under DREAM Act bills in the 111th Congress that would have granted conditional LPR status, the time spent in conditional status under the House-approved DREAM Act language (during which the aliens would have been conditional nonimmigrants) would not have counted for naturalization purposes.

Like other DREAM Act bills in the 111th Congress, the House-approved DREAM Act amendment to H.R. 5281 would have placed restrictions on the eligibility of aliens who adjusted status under its provisions for federal student financial aid under Title IV of the Higher Education Act of 1965, as amended (see "Higher Education Benefits and Immigration Status"). Aliens granted conditional nonimmigrant status or LPR status would have been eligible for student loans, federal work-study programs, and services (such as counseling, tutorial services, and mentoring), subject to the applicable requirements. Unlike other LPRs, they would not have been eligible for federal Pell Grants or federal supplemental educational opportunity grants.

The House-approved version of the DREAM Act also contained provisions on the treatment for other purposes of aliens who were granted conditional nonimmigrant status or LPR status under the bill. It provided that conditional nonimmigrants would have been considered lawfully present for all purposes except for provisions in the Patient Protection and Affordable Care Act concerning premium tax credits and cost sharing subsidies.[53] It also provided that aliens who adjusted to LPR status under the bill would have been deemed to have completed the five-year period required for LPR eligibility for certain types of federal public assistance, as established by the Personal Responsibility and Work Opportunity Reconciliation Act of 1996.[54]

H.R. 1751

The American Dream Act (H.R. 1751), as introduced by Representative Berman, would have repealed IIRIRA Section 505 and thereby eliminated this restriction on state provision of postsecondary educational benefits to unauthorized aliens. It likewise would have enabled eligible unauthorized students to adjust to LPR status in the United States through the cancellation of removal procedure. Under H.R. 1751, aliens could have applied for cancellation of removal without first being placed in removal proceedings, and there would have been no limit on the number of aliens who could be granted cancellation of removal/adjustment of status.

To be eligible for cancellation of removal/adjustment of status under H.R. 1751, an alien would have had to demonstrate that he or she: had been physically present in the United States for a continuous period of not less than five years immediately preceding the date of enactment; had not yet reached age 16 at the time of initial entry; had been a person of good moral character since the time of application; and was not inadmissible or deportable on INA criminal, security, or smuggling grounds. The bill also would have required the alien to demonstrate that he or she had been admitted to an institution of higher education in the United States, or had earned a high school diploma or the equivalent in the United States. Unlike under most other DREAM Act bills in the 111th Congress, however, H.R. 1751 would not have required the alien to show that he or she was under a particular age on the date of enactment. H.R. 1751 also provided for expedited processing of applications without an additional fee.

Aliens granted cancellation of removal under H.R. 1751 would have been adjusted initially to conditional permanent resident status. Such conditional status would have been valid for six years and would have been subject to termination. The time an alien spent as a conditional LPR would have counted for naturalization purposes. Under H.R. 1751, however, the condition on the LPR status would have needed to be removed before the alien could apply for naturalization.

To have the condition removed and become a full-fledged LPR, an alien would have had to apply during a specified period and meet additional requirements. Among these requirements, the alien would have had to demonstrate good moral character during the period of conditional permanent residence; could not have abandoned his or her U.S. residence; and would have needed either to have earned a degree from an institution of higher education (or to have completed at least two years in a bachelor's or higher degree program) in the United States, or to have served in the uniformed services for at least two years.

H.R. 1751 would have placed temporary restrictions on the eligibility of aliens who adjusted to LPR status under its provisions for federal student financial aid under Title IV of the Higher Education Act of 1965, as amended. Aliens adjusting status under the bill would have been eligible for student loans, federal work-study programs, and services, but they would not have been eligible for federal Pell Grants and federal supplemental educational opportunity grants while in conditional permanent resident status. Once the conditional basis was removed and they became full-fledged LPRs, these restrictions would no longer have applied and they would have been eligible for grants. By contrast, under the House-approved version of the DREAM Act and the various Senate bills, aliens who obtained full-fledged LPR status would have remained ineligible for grants.

H.R. 6327

The Citizenship and Service Act of 2010 (H.R. 6327), introduced by Representative Charles Djou, was similar to H.R. 1751 in many respects but noticeably different than that bill in others. Like some other DREAM Act bills but unlike H.R. 1751, H.R. 6327 would not have repealed IIRIRA Section 505. In addition, unlike all the other DREAM Act bills in the 111th Congress discussed here, H.R. 6327 would have required eligible aliens to serve in the uniformed services for at least two years in order to become full-fledged LPRs. Higher education would not have been an alternative to this service requirement under H.R. 6327.

Like H.R. 1751, H.R. 6327 would have enabled eligible unauthorized students to adjust to LPR status in the United States through the cancellation of removal procedure. Aliens could have applied for cancellation of removal without first being placed in removal proceedings, and there would have been no limit on the number of aliens who could be granted cancellation of removal/ adjustment of status.

To be eligible for cancellation of removal/adjustment of status under H.R. 6327, an alien would have had to demonstrate that he or she had been physically present in the United States for a continuous period of not less than five years immediately preceding the date of enactment, had not yet reached age 16 at the time of initial entry, and had been a person of good moral character since the time of application. The alien also would have had to demonstrate that he or she had been admitted to an institution of higher education in the United States, or had earned a high school diploma or the equivalent in the United States.

As under H.R. 1751, an alien applying for cancellation of removal/adjustment of status under H.R. 6327 would have had to demonstrate that he or she was not inadmissible or deportable on INA criminal, security, or smuggling grounds. Also like H.R. 1751, H.R. 6327 provided for expedited processing of applications without an additional fee.

Aliens granted cancellation of removal under H.R. 6327, as under H.R. 1751, would have been adjusted initially to conditional permanent resident status. Such conditional status would have been valid for six years and would have been subject to termination. The time an alien spent as a conditional LPR would have counted for naturalization purposes, but the conditional basis would have had to be removed before the alien could apply to naturalize.

To have the condition removed and become a full-fledged LPR, an alien would have had to apply during a specified period and meet additional requirements. Among these requirements, the alien would have had to have demonstrated good moral character during the period of conditional permanent residence; could not have abandoned his or her U.S. residence; and would have needed to have served in the uniformed services for at least two years. Unlike the other DREAM Act bills in the 111th Congress, H.R. 6327 would not have offered conditional residents the option of completing at least two years of higher education as an alternative to serving in the uniformed services.

H.R. 6327, like H.R. 1751, would have placed temporary restrictions on the eligibility of aliens who adjusted to LPR status under its provisions for federal student financial aid under Title IV of the Higher Education Act of 1965, as amended. Aliens adjusting status under the bill would have been ineligible for federal Pell Grants and federal supplemental educational opportunity grants while in conditional permanent resident status. Once the conditional basis was removed and they became full-fledged LPRs, these restrictions would no longer have applied.

S. 729 and S. 3827

S. 729, the DREAM Act of 2009, and S. 3827, the DREAM Act of 2010, were highly similar bills introduced by Senator Durbin. Differences between S. 729 and S. 3827, as discussed below, concerned the applicable grounds of inadmissibility and the application process under the bills.

Both S. 729 and S. 3827 would have repealed IIRIRA Section 505 and thereby eliminated this restriction on state provision of postsecondary educational benefits to unauthorized aliens. These bills also would have enabled eligible unauthorized students to adjust to LPR status in the United States through cancellation of removal. S. 729 and S. 3827 would have enabled aliens to affirmatively apply for cancellation of removal without first being placed in removal proceedings, and they would have placed no limit on the number of aliens who could be granted cancellation of removal/adjustment of status.

To be eligible for cancellation of removal/adjustment of status under S. 729 and S. 3827, an alien would have had to demonstrate that he or she had been physically present in the United States for a continuous period of not less than five years immediately preceding the date of enactment of the act; had not yet reached age 16 at the time of initial entry; had been a person of good moral character since the time of application; and had not yet reached age 35 on the date of enactment. The alien also would have had to demonstrate that he or she had been admitted to an institution of higher education in the United States, or had earned a high school diploma or the equivalent in the United States.

Under both bills, the alien could not have been inadmissible on INA criminal, security, smuggling, or international child abduction grounds and could not have been deportable on INA criminal, security, or smuggling grounds; S. 3827 also would have made applicable the INA ground of inadmissibility barring practicing polygamists. In addition, under both bills, the alien would have had to show that he or she had never been under a final administrative or judicial order of exclusion, deportation, or removal, with some exceptions.

S. 729 and S. 3827 included some different language concerning the application process. S. 729 included a provision, not included in S. 3827, to consider applications on an expedited basis without charging an additional fee. S. 3827 included a provision, not included in S. 729, establishing a deadline for submitting initial cancellation of removal/adjustment of status applications.

Aliens granted cancellation of removal under S. 729 or S. 3827 would have been adjusted initially to conditional permanent resident status. Such conditional status would have been valid for six years and would have been subject to termination. To have the condition removed and become a full-fledged LPR, an alien would have had to submit an application during a specified period and meet additional requirements. Among these requirements, the alien would have needed to have demonstrated good moral character during the period of conditional permanent residence; could not have abandoned his or her U.S. residence; and would have needed either to have earned a degree from an institution of higher education (or to have completed at least two years in a bachelor's or higher degree program) in the United States, or to have served in the uniformed services for at least two years.

The time an alien spent as a conditional LPR would have counted for naturalization purposes under S. 729 and S. 3827. Under both bills, however, the condition on the LPR status would have to have been removed before an alien could apply for naturalization.

S. 729 and S. 3827 would have placed restrictions on the eligibility of aliens who adjusted to LPR status under their provisions for federal student financial aid under Title IV of the Higher Education Act of 1965, as amended. Aliens adjusting status under S. 729 or S. 3827 would have been eligible only for student loans, federal work-study programs, and services (such as counseling, tutorial services, and mentoring), subject to the applicable requirements. Unlike other LPRs, they would have been ineligible for federal Pell Grants or federal supplemental educational opportunity grants.

S. 3962 and S. 3963

S. 3962 and S. 3963 were two highly similar bills introduced by Senator Durbin, both entitled the DREAM Act of 2010. They differed from one another with respect to the cutoff age for eligibility for cancellation of removal/adjustment of status. S. 3962 and S. 3963 were also similar to S. 3827, another version of the DREAM Act of 2010, discussed in the preceding section. The main difference between S. 3962 and S. 3963 on the one hand and S. 3827 on the other was that the former bills would not have repealed IIRIRA Section 505 and thus would not have eliminated this statutory restriction on state provision of postsecondary educational benefits to unauthorized aliens.

S. 3962 and S. 3963 would have enabled eligible unauthorized students to adjust to LPR status in the United States through cancellation of removal. Both bills would have enabled aliens to affirmatively apply for cancellation of removal without first being placed in removal proceedings, and they would have placed no limit on the number of aliens who could be granted cancellation of removal/adjustment of status. There would have been a deadline for submitting initial cancellation of removal/adjustment of status applications.

To be eligible for cancellation of removal/adjustment of status under S. 3962 and S. 3963, an alien would have had to demonstrate that he or she had been physically present in the United States for a continuous period of not less than five years immediately preceding the date of enactment of the act, had not yet reached age 16 at the time of initial entry, and had been a person of good moral character since the time of application. Both bills also included an eligibility requirement concerning the age of the alien on the date of enactment of the legislation. Under S. 3962, the alien would have had to demonstrate that he or she had not yet reached age 35 on the date of enactment. Under S. 3963, the alien would have had to demonstrate that he or she had not yet reached age 30 on the date of enactment. Under both bills, the alien also would have had to demonstrate that he or she had been admitted to an institution of higher education in the United States, or had earned a high school diploma or the equivalent in the United States.

As under S. 3827, an alien applying for relief under S. 3962 and S. 3963 would have had to show that he or she was not inadmissible on INA criminal, security, smuggling, polygamy, or international child abduction grounds, and was not deportable on INA criminal, security, or smuggling grounds. The alien also would have had to show that he or she had never been under a final administrative or judicial order of exclusion, deportation, or removal, with some exceptions.

Aliens granted cancellation of removal under S. 3962 or S. 3963 would have been adjusted initially to conditional permanent resident status. Such conditional status would have been valid for six years and would have been subject to termination. The time an alien spent as a conditional LPR would have counted for naturalization purposes, but the conditional basis would have had to be removed before the alien could apply to naturalize.

To have the condition removed and become a full-fledged LPR, an alien would have had to submit an application during a specified period and meet additional requirements. Among these requirements, the alien would have needed to have demonstrated good moral character during the period of conditional permanent residence; could not have abandoned his or her U.S. residence; and would have needed either to have earned a degree from an institution of higher education (or to have completed at least two years in a bachelor's or higher degree program) in the United States, or to have served in the uniformed services for at least two years.

S. 3962 and S. 3963 would have placed restrictions on the eligibility of aliens who adjusted to LPR status under their provisions for federal student financial aid under Title IV of the Higher Education Act of 1965, as amended. Aliens adjusting status under S. 3962 or S. 3963 would have been eligible only for student loans, federal work-study programs, and services (such as counseling, tutorial services, and mentoring), subject to the applicable requirements. Unlike other LPRs, they would not have been eligible for federal Pell Grants or federal supplemental educational opportunity grants.

S. 3992

S. 3992, another version of the DREAM Act of 2010 introduced by Senator Durbin, would, like the other DREAM Act bills in the 111th Congress, have enabled eligible unauthorized students to adjust to LPR status in the United States. Its legalization provisions were similar to those in the House-approved DREAM Act amendment to H.R. 5281, although there were some differences between the measures. Also like the House-approved amendment, S. 3992 would not have repealed IIRIRA Section 505 and thus would not have eliminated this statutory restriction on state provision of postsecondary educational benefits to unauthorized aliens.

Under S. 3992, as under the House-approved DREAM Act amendment to H.R. 5281, an eligible alien could have gone through the cancellation of removal procedure and been granted conditional *nonimmigrant* status. An alien could have affirmatively applied for cancellation of removal without first being placed in removal proceedings, and there would have been a deadline for submitting initial cancellation of removal applications. There would have been no limit on the number of aliens who could be granted cancellation of removal under S. 3992.

To be eligible for cancellation of removal/conditional nonimmigrant status under S. 3992, an alien would have had to meet requirements similar to those in the House-approved version of the DREAM Act. The alien would have had to demonstrate that he or she had been physically present in the United States for a continuous period of not less than five years immediately preceding the date of enactment of the legislation, had not yet reached age 16 at the time of initial entry, had been a person of good moral character since the date of initial entry, and was younger than age 30 on the date of enactment. The alien also would have had to demonstrate that he or she had been admitted to an institution of higher education in the United States, or had earned a high school diploma or the equivalent in the United States, and that he or she had never been under a final administrative or judicial order of exclusion, deportation, or removal, with some exceptions. Unlike under the House-approved DREAM Act amendment to H.R. 5281, there would have been no surcharges on applications under S. 3992.

The same grounds of inadmissibility and deportability would have applied under S. 3992 as under the House-approved DREAM Act language. An alien applying for relief under this bill would have had to show that he or she was not inadmissible on INA health-related, criminal, security, public charge, smuggling, student visa abuse, citizenship ineligibility, polygamy, international child abduction, or unlawful voting grounds, and was not deportable on INA criminal, security, smuggling, marriage fraud, public charge, or unlawful voting grounds.[55] Applicants would further have needed to: satisfy requirements concerning convictions for offenses under federal or state law; submit biometric and biographic data, which would have been used to conduct background checks; and register under the Military Selective Service Act, if applicable.

Aliens whose removal was cancelled under S. 3992 would have been granted conditional nonimmigrant status. Such conditional status would have been valid for 10 years (compared to H.R. 5281's initial period of five years, which could have been extended for a second five-year period) and would have been subject to termination.

For adjustment to LPR status, the conditional nonimmigrant would have had to submit an application during a specified period and meet requirements similar to those in other DREAM Act bills. Among these requirements, the alien would have needed to have demonstrated good moral character during the period of conditional nonimmigrant status; could not have abandoned his or her U.S. residence; and would have needed either to have earned a degree from an institution of higher education (or to have completed at least two years in a bachelor's or higher degree program) in the United States, or to have served in the Armed Forces for at least two years. Other requirements included satisfaction of the English language and civic requirements for naturalization, payment of federal taxes, submission of biometric and biographic data, and completion of background checks. There would have been no limitation on the number of individuals eligible for adjustment of status under S. 3992.

Aliens who adjusted status under S. 3992 and met other requirements would have been eligible for naturalization after three years in LPR status. The time spent in conditional status under S. 3992, as under the House-approved DREAM Act amendment to H.R. 5281 (during which the aliens would have been conditional nonimmigrants, as opposed to conditional LPRs under the other DREAM Act bills), would not have counted for naturalization purposes.

Like the House-approved DREAM Act amendment to H.R. 5281, S. 3992 would have placed restrictions on the eligibility of aliens who adjusted status under its provisions for federal student financial aid under Title IV of the Higher Education Act of 1965, as amended. Aliens granted conditional nonimmigrant status or LPR status under S. 3992 would have been eligible for student loans, federal work-study programs, and services (such as counseling, tutorial services, and mentoring), subject to the applicable requirements. Unlike other LPRs, they would not have been eligible for federal Pell Grants or federal supplemental educational opportunity grants.

S. 3992 also contained provisions like those in the House-approved DREAM Act amendment to H.R. 5281 on the treatment for other purposes of aliens who were granted conditional nonimmigrant status or LPR status under the bill. It provided that conditional nonimmigrants would have been considered lawfully present for all purposes except for provisions in the Patient Protection and Affordable Care Act concerning premium tax credits and cost sharing subsidies. It also provided that aliens who adjusted to LPR status under the bill would have been deemed to have completed the five-year period required for LPR eligibility for certain types of federal public assistance, as established by the Personal Responsibility and Work Opportunity Reconciliation Act of 1996.

End Notes

[1] This report generally describes beneficiaries of the DREAM Act as "students" as a convenient shorthand, following common practice. As a technical matter, however, an individual would not have to be a currently enrolled student in order to be granted immigration relief under the DREAM Act. The eligibility requirements under the various DREAM Act proposals are detailed in this report.

[2] For a discussion of the legal basis for the provision of free public education, see CRS Report RS22500, Unauthorized Alien Students, Higher Education, and In-State Tuition Rates: A Legal Analysis, by Jody Feder.

[3] IIRIRA is Division C of P.L. 104-208, September 30, 1996. The provision is §505.

[4] Unauthorized alien students are distinct from a group commonly referred to as foreign students. Like unauthorized alien students, foreign students are foreign nationals. Unlike unauthorized alien students, however, foreign students enter the United States legally on nonimmigrant (temporary) visas in order to study at U.S. institutions.

[5] Legal permanent residents, also known as immigrants and green card holders, are noncitizens who are legally authorized to reside permanently in the United States.

[6] The HEA is P.L. 89-329, November 8, 1965, 20 U.S.C. §1001 et seq. Section 484(a)(5) sets forth immigration-related eligibility requirements for federal student financial aid, and §484(g) requires the U.S. Department of Education to verify the immigration status of applicants for federal financial aid. Also see U.S. Department of Education, Office of Federal Student Aid, Federal Student Aid Handbook 2012-2013, Volume 1 (Student Eligibility), Chapter 2 (Citizenship), http://ifap.ed.gov/fsahandbook/attachments/ 1213 FSAHbkVol1Ch2.pdf.

[7] No implementing regulations on §505 have been issued.

[8] U.S. Congress, House Conference Committee, Illegal Immigration Reform and Immigrant Responsibility Act of 1996, conference report to accompany H.R. 2202, 104th Cong., 2nd sess., H.Rept. 104-828, p. 240.

[9] See, for example, Dawn Konet, "Unauthorized Youths and Higher Education: The Ongoing Debate," Migration Information Source, Migration Policy Institute, September 2007, http://www.migrationinformation.org/Feature/ display.cfm?ID=642.

[10] Cal. Educ. Code §68130.5. The law does not apply to the University of California system.

[11] For additional information, see CRS Report RS22500, Unauthorized Alien Students, Higher Education, and In-State Tuition Rates: A Legal Analysis.

[12] U.S. Department of Homeland Security, Memorandum to David V. Aguilar, Acting Commissioner, U.S. Customs and Border Protection, Alejandro Mayorkas, Director, U.S. Citizenship and Immigration Services, John Morton, Director, U.S. Immigration and Customs Enforcement, from Janet Napolitano, Secretary of Homeland Security, Exercising Prosecutorial Discretion with Respect to Individuals Who Came to the United States as Children, June 15, 2012, http://www.dhs.gov/xlibrary/assets/s1-exercising-prosecutorial-discretion-individuals-who-came-to-us-aschildren.pdf (hereinafter cited as DHS, Exercising Prosecutorial Discretion, June 15, 2012).

[13] Deferred action is "a discretionary determination to defer removal action of an individual as an act of prosecutorial discretion." U.S. Department of Homeland Security, U.S. Citizenship and Immigration Services, Consideration of Deferred Action for Childhood Arrivals Process, Frequently Asked Questions, http://www.uscis.gov/humanitarian/ consideration-deferred-action-childhood-arrivals-process/frequently-asked-questions. For additional information on prosecutorial discretion and deferred action, see CRS Congressional Distribution Memorandum, Analysis of June 15, 2012 DHS Memorandum, "Exercising Prosecutorial Discretion with Respect to Individuals Who Came to the United States as Children," by Andorra Bruno, Todd Garvey, Kate Manuel, and Ruth Ellen Wasem (available to congressional staff from the authors).

[14] DHS, Exercising Prosecutorial Discretion, June 15, 2012, p. 3. The memorandum states: "This memorandum confers no substantive right, immigration status or pathway to citizenship. Only the Congress, acting through its legislative authority, can confer these rights. It remains for the executive branch, however, to set forth policy for the exercise of discretion within the framework of the existing law."

[15] Jeanne Batalova and Margie McHugh, DREAM vs. Reality: An Analysis of Potential DREAM Act Beneficiaries, Migration Policy Institute, July 2010, http://www. migrationpolicy.org (hereinafter cited as MPI, DREAM vs. Reality). MPI is a self-described independent, nonpartisan, nonprofit think tank dedicated to the analysis of international migration.

[16] See description of S. 729 in the Appendix.

[17] MPI, DREAM vs. Reality, p. 17.

[18] Steven A. Camarota, Estimating the Impact of the DREAM Act, Center for Immigration Studies, December 2010, http://www.cis.org. CIS is a self-described independent, non-partisan, non-profit research organization with a "low-immigration, pro-immigrant" vision.

[19] See "S. 729 and S. 3827" in the Appendix.

[20] Jeanne Batalova and Michelle Mittelstadt, Relief from Deportation: Demographic Profile of the DREAMers Potentially Eligible under the Deferred Action Policy, Migration Policy Institute, August 2012. These estimates update earlier June 2012 MPI estimates that put the potentially eligible DACA population at 1.4 million.

[21] Data available at http://www.uscis.gov.

[22] See "House-approved DREAM Act Language and H.R. 6497" in the Appendix.

[23] As set forth in INA §244, TPS is blanket relief that may be granted under the following conditions: there is ongoing armed conflict posing serious threat to personal safety; a foreign state requests TPS because it temporarily cannot handle the return of nationals due to environmental disaster; or there are extraordinary and temporary conditions in a foreign state that prevent aliens from returning provided that granting TPS is consistent with U.S. national interests. See CRS Report RS20844, Temporary Protected Status: Current Immigration Policy and Issues, by Ruth Ellen Wasem and Karma Ester.

[24] The INA grounds of inadmissibility are in INA §212(a). See CRS Report R41104, Immigration Visa Issuances and Grounds for Exclusion: Policy and Trends, by Ruth Ellen Wasem.

[25] Unlike DREAM Act bills in prior Congresses, S. 952 did not specify grounds of deportability that would have applied to aliens seeking relief. The INA grounds of deportability are in INA §237(a).

[26] The Secretary of Homeland Security would have had the authority to waive specified grounds for humanitarian, family unity, or public interest purposes.

[27] This age five cutoff was a departure from past DREAM Act bills, which typically had limited protections from removal to potential beneficiaries who were at least age 12.

[28] As defined in Section 101(a) of Title 10 of the U.S. Code, the term uniformed services means the Armed Forces (Army, Navy, Air Force, Marine Corps, and Coast Guard); the commissioned corps of the National Oceanic and Atmospheric Administration; and the commissioned corps of the Public Health Service.

[29] Naturalization is the process through which an LPR becomes a U.S. citizen.

[30] The Secretary of Homeland Security would have had the authority to waive the criminal grounds for humanitarian, family unity, or public interest purposes.

[31] See "House-approved DREAM Act Language and H.R. 6497" in the Appendix.

[32] Under H.R. 1842, an alien would have had to be age 32 or younger; under S. 952, an alien would have had to be age 35 or younger.

[33] The Secretary of Homeland Security would have had the authority to waive some of these grounds of inadmissibility and deportability for humanitarian, family unity, or public interest purposes.

[34] The term Armed Forces, as defined in Section 101(a) of Title 10 of the U.S. Code, means the Army, Navy, Air Force, Marine Corps, and Coast Guard.

[35] P.L. 111-148, March 23, 2010.

[36] For information on the PPACA provisions, see CRS Report R41714, Treatment of Noncitizens Under the Patient Protection and Affordable Care Act, by Alison Siskin.

[37] PRWORA is P.L. 104-193, August 22, 1996. For information on current eligibility policy, see CRS Report RL33809, Noncitizen Eligibility for Federal Public Assistance: Policy Overview and Trends, by Ruth Ellen Wasem.

[38] See "House-approved DREAM Act Language and H.R. 6497" in the Appendix.

[39] Under H.R. 1842, an alien would have had to be age 32 or younger; under S. 952, an alien would have had to be age 35 or younger.

[40] The Secretary of Homeland Security would have had the authority to waive some of these grounds of inadmissibility and deportability for humanitarian, family unity, or public interest purposes.

[41] See CRS Report R43097, Comprehensive Immigration Reform in the 113th Congress: Major Provisions in Senate-Passed S. 744, by Marc R. Rosenblum and Ruth Ellen Wasem.

[42] Under both bills, there would be a separate legalization program for certain agricultural workers.

[43] Unlike other DREAM Act bills, S. 744 and H.R. 15 would not use the cancellation of removal procedure to confer legal status on beneficiaries.

[44] Certain other grounds would apply in specified circumstances. The Secretary of Homeland Security would have the authority to waive some applicable grounds of inadmissibility for humanitarian, family unity, or public interest purposes.

[45] For a discussion of these protections, see CRS Report R43097, Comprehensive Immigration Reform in the 113th Congress: Major Provisions in Senate-Passed S. 744.

[46] Both bills would add a new section (245D) to the INA.

[47] S. 744 and H.R. 15 also would bar RPIs from receiving certain federally provided benefits. See CRS Report R43097, Comprehensive Immigration Reform in the 113th Congress: Major Provisions in Senate-Passed S. 744.

[48] Under the INA, with some exceptions, an alien must be an LPR for five years before he or she can naturalize.

[49] For pro and con arguments, see, for example, Jerry Gonzalez and Phil Kent, "Should Congress Pass DREAM Act for Immigrant Children?," Atlanta Journal-Constitution, November 23, 2010; Stacy Teicher Khadaroo, "Why DREAM Act Passed House, But May Fall in Senate,"

Christian Science Monitor, December 9, 2010; and Beth Brown, "DREAM Act Youths Might Be Worth Billions to Texas," San Antonio Express-News, October 31, 2012.

[50] For legislation introduced in earlier Congresses, see archived CRS Report RL31365, Unauthorized Alien Students: Legislation in the 107th and 108th Congresses, by Andorra Bruno and Jeffrey J. Kuenzi.

[51] In addition, on December 9, 2010, following House action on H.R. 5281, there was another DREAM Act-related vote in the Senate. That day, the Senate voted, 59-40, to table a motion to proceed to a Senate DREAM Act bill, S. 3992. DREAM Act supporters voted for the tabling motion in an effort to clear the way for the Senate to consider the House-approved DREAM Act amendment to H.R. 5281.

[52] The Secretary of Homeland Security would have had the authority to waive some of these grounds of inadmissibility and deportability for humanitarian, family unity, or public interest purposes.

[53] For information on the PPACA provisions, see CRS Report R41714, Treatment of Noncitizens Under the Patient Protection and Affordable Care Act.

[54] For information on current eligibility policy, see CRS Report RL33809, Noncitizen Eligibility for Federal Public Assistance: Policy Overview and Trends.

[55] The Secretary of Homeland Security would have the authority to waive some of these grounds for humanitarian, family unity, or public interest purposes.

In: Unaccompanied Alien Children in the U.S. ISBN: 978-1-63321-832-1
Editor: Paul Snider

Chapter 5

COMPREHENSIVE IMMIGRATION REFORM IN THE 113TH CONGRESS: SHORT SUMMARY OF SENATE-PASSED S. 744*

Marc R. Rosenblum and Ruth Ellen Wasem

SUMMARY

For several years, some Members of Congress have favored "comprehensive immigration reform" (CIR), a label that commonly refers to omnibus legislation that includes increased border security and immigration enforcement, expanded employment eligibility verification, revision of nonimmigrant visas and legal permanent immigration, and legalization for some unauthorized aliens residing in the country. The omnibus legislative approach contrasts with incremental revisions of the Immigration and Nationality Act (INA) and other immigration laws that would address some but not all of these elements, and with sequential reforms that would tackle border security and interior enforcement provisions prior to revising legal immigration or enacting legalization pathways.

Leaders in both chambers have identified immigration as a legislative priority in the 113th Congress. While the House Committee on the Judiciary has ordered reported several distinct pieces of legislation that

---

* This is an edited, reformatted and augmented version of a Congressional Research Service publication R43099, prepared for Members and Committees of Congress, dated July 10, 2013.

aim to reform immigration law thus far in the 113th Congress, the debate in the Senate has focused on a single CIR bill: the Border Security, Economic Opportunity, and Immigration Modernization Act (S. 744). This report briefly summarizes major provisions of S. 744, which the Senate amended and passed by a yea-nay vote of 68-32 on June 27, 2013.

CRS's analysis focuses on eight major policy areas that encompass the U.S. immigration debate: comprehensive reform "triggers" and funding; border security; interior enforcement; employment eligibility verification and worksite enforcement; legalization of unauthorized aliens; immigrant visas; nonimmigrant visas; and humanitarian provisions.

This report provides a concise summary of S. 744 related to each of these issues.

For a number of years, some Members of Congress have favored "comprehensive immigration reform" (CIR), a label that commonly refers to omnibus legislation that includes increased border security and immigration enforcement, expanded employment eligibility verification, revision of nonimmigrant visas and legal permanent immigration, and legalization for some unauthorized aliens residing in the country. Other Members of Congress may favor addressing these issues sequentially (e.g., by implementing enforcement provisions prior to legalization), and/or may disagree with the legalization and increased legal immigration provisions that have been features of major CIR bills. Still others may be interested in legislating on some elements of CIR but not others.

Leaders in both chambers have identified immigration as a legislative priority in the 113th Congress. While the House Committee on the Judiciary has ordered reported several distinct pieces of legislation that aim to reform immigration law thus far in the 113th Congress, the debate in the Senate has focused on a single CIR bill: the Border Security, Economic Opportunity, and Immigration Modernization Act (S. 744), which was reported by the Senate Judiciary Committee May 28, 2013, and was amended during three weeks of floor debate before being passed by the Senate on a yea-nay vote of 68-32 on June 27, 2013.

This report succinctly summarizes major provisions of S. 744, as passed by the Senate. CRS's analysis focuses on eight major policy areas that encompass the U.S. immigration debate: comprehensive reform "triggers" and funding; border security; interior enforcement; employment eligibility verification and worksite enforcement; legalization of unauthorized aliens; immigrant visas; nonimmigrant visas; and humanitarian provisions.

COMPREHENSIVE REFORM "TRIGGERS" AND FUNDING

Some Members of Congress have raised concerns about proposals for comprehensive immigration reform on the grounds that the "bargain" some people see at the heart of such reform—tougher enforcement on the one hand and legalization plus visa reforms on the other— may be difficult to enforce. To allay the concerns that legalization would go forward without increased enforcement, the first sections of Senate-passed S. 744 would make implementation of certain enforcement provisions pre-conditions (or "triggers") for the bill's legalization provisions. These legalization triggers were substantially broadened during the Senate floor debate in an effort to strengthen the bill's enforcement provisions. In addition, as passed by the Senate, S. 744 would authorize $51.8 billion in direct spending (i.e., spending that would go into effect without further congressional action) for certain border security and immigration enforcement expenses, for initial administrative and startup costs related to the bill, and for workforce training.[1]

BORDER SECURITY

Border security is a core element of the Department of Homeland Security's (DHS's) effort to control unauthorized migration,[2] and S. 744 includes a number of sections designed to better secure the Southern border. DHS would be required to submit to Congress a "Comprehensive Southern Border Security Strategy" and to establish a "Southern Border Fencing Strategy," both within 180 days of enactment, and to begin implementing the Comprehensive Security Strategy immediately upon its submission. As amended during the Senate floor debate, the bill includes a detailed sector-by-sector list of technological assets to be included as minimum requirements in the Comprehensive Security Strategy; and it requires that the Fencing Strategy identify where 700 miles of fencing should be deployed along the Southern border. The bill would direct DHS to hire 3,500 additional CBP officers at ports of entry and, as amended on the Senate floor, would require CBP to deploy 19,200 additional Border Patrol agents to the Southern border.

In addition to these increases in border security personnel, equipment, and infrastructure, S. 744 would provide DHS with authority to waive certain restrictions on fencing and border infrastructure; give DHS access to certain federal lands; modify certain immigration-related crimes and increase border prosecutions; and strengthen the existing electronic entry-exit system. Of the direct spending authorized by the bill, about $45 billion would be designated for border enforcement activities, and $500 million would be designated to reimburse air and sea carriers for the collection of electronic exit data. The bill also includes a number of provisions to strengthen oversight of border security activities.

INTERIOR ENFORCEMENT

The immigration rules established by the Immigration and Nationality Act (INA) are supplemented by an enforcement regime to deter and punish violations of those rules. Violations may be subject to criminal penalties, civil fines, and/or may be grounds for an alien to be removed from the country.

Senate-passed S. 744 would amend the INA to create additional grounds of inadmissibility and deportability, while broadening judges' discretion to waive some of these grounds. For certain immigration offenses, the bill would increase civil and misdemeanor penalties for first-time offenses and impose felony penalties when aggravating circumstances exist. The bill would amend INA provisions on unlawful reentry to increase criminal penalties. S. 744 would provide additional resources to immigration courts and would encourage alternatives to detention and strengthen detention standards and congressional oversight of immigrant detention. Special provisions would be included to protect children who are affected by immigration enforcement.

EMPLOYMENT ELIGIBILITY VERIFICATION AND WORKSITE ENFORCEMENT

Under current law, it is illegal for an employer to knowingly hire, recruit or refer for a fee, or continue to employ an alien who is not authorized to be so employed; but enforcement of these provisions has been problematic.[3]

S. 744 would strike and re-write the employment verification and worksite enforcement provisions of the INA, taking steps to strengthen document integrity and imposing a new requirement to be phased in over time that all employers use an electronic eligibility verification system similar to the current E-Verify system.[4] The bill would increase civil and criminal penalties against employers who violate these provisions, and would include additional provisions designed to limit the burden on employers that would result from these changes, and to protect the rights of U.S. citizens and other lawful workers. Of the direct spending authorized by the bill, $750 million would be designated for DHS to implement the mandatory electronic employment verification system to be used by all employers.

LEGALIZATION OF UNAUTHORIZED ALIENS

How to address the unauthorized alien population in the United States is a key and controversial issue in comprehensive immigration reform.[5]

Senate-passed S. 744 would establish a general legalization program for most unauthorized aliens in the United States. The bill would establish a new multi-step, multi-year process that would enable eligible unauthorized aliens—after DHS certifies that the enforcement triggers have been satisfied—to transition into a provisional legal status and ultimately to lawful permanent residence. Special pathways would be created for certain aliens who entered the country as children[6] and for agricultural workers.[7] In general, aliens who qualify for the initial legalization program eventually could have an opportunity to apply to become legal permanent residents (LPRs).

IMMIGRANT VISAS

Immigrants are persons admitted as legal permanent residents (LPRs)[8] of the United States. Under current law, permanent admissions are subject to a complex set of numerical limits and preference categories that give priority for admission on the basis of family relationships, an offer or employment in the United States, and geographic diversity of sending countries.[9]

Senate-passed S. 744 would substantially revise future flows of immigrant visas. Spouses and children of LPRs would be reclassified as immediate relatives, and not subject to numerical limits. Certain high skilled employment-based immigrants would be exempted from numerical limits, notably aliens with advanced degrees in science, technology, engineering, or mathematics (STEM) fields, along with the spouses and children of employment-based immigrants. Two new "merit-based" systems also would be established: one to admit workers based on their employment skills, and the other to admit persons in the existing visa backlog, adult siblings who apply before that visa is eliminated, and ultimately unauthorized aliens adjusting to legal permanent status under S. 744. The overall per-country limit would increase to 15% for family-based immigrants, and would be eliminated for employment-based immigrants. And S. 744 also would modify investor visas, establish new programs to promote immigrant integration, and make several other changes to immigrant visa policy. The current diversity visa lottery and family fourth preference visa (for adult siblings of U.S. citizens) would be phased out.

NONIMMIGRANT VISAS

Nonimmigrants—such as tourists, foreign students, diplomats, temporary workers, cultural exchange participants, or intracompany business personnel—are admitted for a specific purpose and a temporary period of time.[10]

Senate-passed S. 744 would revise and expand nonimmigrant (i.e., temporary immigration) programs for high- and low-skilled workers, as well as for tourists, students, and other nonimmigrants. The bill would increase the cap on professional specialty workers (H-1B workers), while also imposing new requirements on businesses that employ H-1B workers, as well as those that employ intra-company transferees (L visas). Reforms would be made to the existing H-2B program for lower-skilled non-agricultural workers in temporary or seasonal employment, while the H-2A program for agricultural workers would be phased out.[11] New nonimmigrant visa programs would be established for lower skilled agricultural and nonagricultural workers that would be more flexible for employers, while also expanding certain rights for workers. Additional nonimmigrant visa changes would facilitate temporary immigration by doctors, investors, and aliens from certain countries with U.S. trade agreements; encourage tourism within the United States; and strengthen oversight of foreign students, among other changes.

HUMANITARIAN PROVISIONS

The United States has long held to the principle that it will not return a foreign national to a country where his life or freedom would be threatened. This principle is embodied in several provisions of the INA, most notably in provisions defining refugees and asylees.[12] Current law also includes provisions to protect certain other humanitarian populations.

Senate-passed S. 744 would increase the flexibility of asylum and refugee provisions several ways, including by expanding the time period for an alien to apply for asylum and expanding certain benefits to families of asylees. Other changes would tighten refugee and asylum laws and would be especially aimed at national security concerns. The bill also would include provisions to combat human trafficking, to protect trafficking victims, and to grant legal status to certain battered spouses and children.

CONGRESSIONAL BUDGET OFFICE ANALYSIS OF S. 744

The Congressional Budget Office (CBO) projects that the changes to immigration resulting from S. 744 as passed by the Senate would result in a net increase of 9.6 million LPRs in the first decade after enactment. Although CBO has observed the long-standing convention of not incorporating macroeconomic effects in cost estimates, CBO and the Joint Committee on Taxation "relaxed that assumption by incorporating in this cost estimate their projections of the direct effects of the act on the U.S. population, employment, and taxable compensation." The increase in the number of legal residents would boost federal revenues, according to CBO, mostly because of the larger size of the labor force. CBO further estimates that the number of legal residents would boost direct spending for federal benefit programs and notes that under S. 744 direct spending for enforcement and other purposes also would increase. As a consequence, CBO estimates that enacting S. 744 as passed by the Senate would "lead to a net savings of about $135 billion over the 2014-2023 period."[13]

End Notes

[1] This figure includes $46.8 billion out of the Comprehensive Immigration Reform (CIR) Trust Fund pursuant to section 6(a) of the Border Security, Economic Opportunity, and Immigration Modernization Act (S. 744); $3 billion out of the CIR Startup Account pursuant to S. 744 §6(b); $500 million out of the Interior Enforcement Account pursuant to S. 744 §3304(f); $20 million pursuant to §4701(j) to establish a Bureau of Immigration and Labor Market Research and $1.5 billion pursuant to §5102 for a Youth Jobs Fund. S. 744 also would authorize additional discretionary spending in various places throughout the bill. For a fuller discussion, see William A. Kandel and Marc R. Rosenblum, "Funding

Accounts, Direct and Discretionary Spending, Fees, and Penalties in S. 744, the Border Security, Economic Opportunity, and Immigration Modernization Act," CRS congressional distribution memorandum available from the authors.

[2] For an overview of current efforts to prevent unauthorized migration at U.S. borders, see CRS Report R42138, Border Security: Immigration Enforcement Between Ports of Entry, by Marc R. Rosenblum.

[3] For an overview of existing employer sanctions provisions, see CRS Report R40002, Immigration-Related Worksite Enforcement: Performance Measures, by Andorra Bruno.

[4] For an overview of the E-Verify program, see CRS Report R40446, Electronic Employment Eligibility Verification, by Andorra Bruno.

[5] For a fuller discussion of these issues, see CRS Report R42958, Unauthorized Aliens: Policy Options for Providing Targeted Immigration Relief, by Andorra Bruno.

[6] Such aliens previously have been the subject of similar stand-alone legislation known as the Development, Relief, and Education for Alien Minors (DREAM) Act; for a fuller discussion see CRS Report RL33863, Unauthorized Alien Students: Issues and "DREAM Act" Legislation, by Andorra Bruno.

[7] Broadly similar provisions have been included in measures introduced regularly in recent Congresses, including in bills known as the Agricultural Job Opportunities, Benefits, and Security Act (AgJOBS Act)

[8] Legal permanent residents (LPRs) are foreign nationals who come to live lawfully and permanent in the United States.

[9] For a fuller discussion, see CRS Report R42866, Permanent Legal Immigration to the United States: Policy Overview, by Ruth Ellen Wasem.

[10] For a fuller discussion of nonimmigrant visas, see CRS Report RL31381, U.S. Immigration Policy on Temporary Admissions, by Ruth Ellen Wasem.

[11] For a fuller discussion of the H-2A and H-2B programs, see CRS Report R42434, Immigration of Temporary Lower-Skilled Workers: Current Policy and Related Issues, by Andorra Bruno.

[12] For a fuller discussion, see For a fuller discussion, see CRS Report RL31269, Refugee Admissions and Resettlement Policy, by Andorra Bruno; and CRS Report R41753, Asylum and "Credible Fear" Issues in U.S. Immigration Policy, by Ruth Ellen Wasem.

[13] Congressional Budget Office, S. 744, Border Security, Economic Opportunity, and Immigration Modernization Act, As passed by the Senate on June 27, 2013, July 3, 2013, http://cbo.gov/publication/44397/.

INDEX

C

D

G

H

I

N

O

P

T

U

V

W

Y